Y0-CJC-818

The Path of Faith

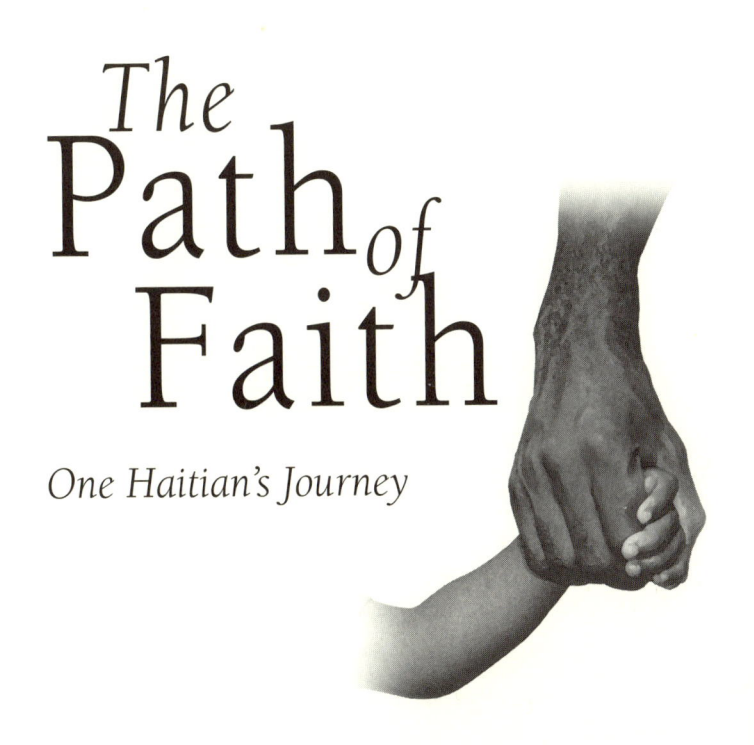

One Haitian's Journey

JOEL BUISSERETH
AND ARLEN MILLER

NOTICE—The value of the Haitian dollar was equal to that of the American dollar until the mid-1980s when the Haitian dollar value lowered about 5% and since then has slowly decreased until today it is about 50% of the American dollar. All mentions of Haitian dollar amounts in this volume are without further explanation in value relative to the American dollar at the time of the occurrence in the story.

Illustrations by PTP

"Father" on page 140, photo courtesy of Darla Yancey Kizer/JB

Map of Haiti by MapArt

All scripture quotations are from the King James Version of the Bible

Cover design by Charity Miller

© August 2001 Palm Tree Press

All rights reserved. No portion of this book may be reproduced by any means, electronic or mechanical, including photocopying, recording, or by any information storage retrieval system, without written permission of the copyright's owner, except for the inclusion of brief quotations for a review.

THE PATH OF FAITH

JOEL BUISSERETH and Arlen Miller

ISBN 0-9709465-0-3 (Regular Edition, paperback)

Send your comments or suggestions to:

palm tree press
4842 Township Road 420
Sugarcreek, Ohio 44681

Printed by Carlisle Printing, Sugarcreek, Ohio

*to my wife, Rachel and the boys,
Samuel, Gardel and Raphael*

This is the story of a young man who started his life in a very poor situation but was determined to do something with his life. He had a good upbringing and learned early to look to God for help and wanted to serve Him!

NELSON ROES
Board Chairman, Son Light Mission, Castorland, New York

Evangelism is the burning passion in Joel's heart and he, like many others, uses different methods to carry that message to a lost and dying world. Joel has learned to use so many vehicles with which to carry the message. But first and foremost is his goal to teach his fellow Haitians to read and write. Not only so they can provide for, and care for, themselves and their families physically but also spiritually. A literate people cannot be easily bought. Joel is claiming Haiti for Christ beginning with his valley of Labaleine.

DARLA YANCEY KIZER, RN
Former Board Member, Christian Fellowship Mission, Sarasota, Florida

---

I think everyone will like to read something like this about a wonderful man of God.

REV. ROLAND JOSEPH, Senior Pastor,
Haitian Ministry Theophile Church in Christ, Atlanta, Georgia

Contents

Foreword vii

Preface ix

Thanks xi

Introduction xiii

Map of Haiti xv

Hurricane Flora 1

And After 5

Childhood 9

Kòvé 35

Sisal 43

The Gospel Comes to Labaleine 47

School 55

Miragoane 67

Port-au-Prince 71

America? 77

Yes, America! 81

Haiti Again 91

Rachel 95

America Again 99

Rachel to America 103

Tifton 105

Kansas 115

School in Labaleine! 121

The News 129

Return 133

Father 141

Back to Georgia 147

Florida 151

Pearl of the Antilles 157

Coffee, Sisal, Goats 159

Back and Forth 163

Perspectives on Haitian Life 167

The Vision 171

Foreword

I was first introduced to a remarkable young man named Joel Buissereth in September 1980. Mennonite Central Committee had asked me to assess the loss of life and property inflicted by Hurricane Allen. Being new in Haiti I was looking for a bilingual guide who knew the back roads of southern Haiti where the storm had struck just days before. So I was in Petionville late one night sitting on Eris and Miriam Labady's patio when my host casually mentioned that he knew someone who could travel with me.

As you read Joel's story, you will realize as I did, that God could not have provided a better companion for my assignment. And so, somewhere between Côtes-de-Fer and Labaleine, over a Land Rover's determined roar as we escaped one mud hole after another, I first heard the story of Hurricane Flora ... and we became lifelong friends.

We have become close friends because Joel has a God-given gift of helping people he meets feel honored, loved, and encouraged. All of the people mentioned in this book would probably describe their relationship with Joel in the same way. His story is a testimony to this special grace that Joel has carried so unselfishly into every relationship. I am humbled again, as I write, realizing that God has allowed me to observe this life of such integrity and utmost sincerity. I am kinder and gentler because I have walked and lived beside Joel.

Of course, Joel's humility has not allowed him to write specifically about the hundreds, probably thousands, of people, Haitians and Americans alike, whose lives have been reoriented as a result of his ministry ... as a teacher, trainer, consultant, pastor, agriculturist, social worker, preacher, and friend. Regardless of his earthly job description, Joel has always found a way to point others to God. May his written story be an inspiration to your own journey toward God.

Joel is quick to say "To God be the glory!" Let me beat him to it by declaring in my American accent, "Gloua a Die! Mesi Jezi!" (Glory to God! Thank you, Jesus)

WALTER SAWATZKY, *Missions Coordinator*
Franconia Mennonite Conference, Souderton, Pennsylvania

Preface

I thank God for this privilege of getting to know Joel in a very personal way while hearing his story firsthand. It has deepened my respect for race, culture, personality, and ethnic backgrounds. I can only believe my life is better because of it. I am awed by all the people that Joel's life has touched and I give my salutations to you, his friends, who have made his story complete. Joel is a man of vision and perspective and worthy of your ear. Praises to God.

ARLEN MILLER

Thanks

A deep feeling of gratitude goes to all who I have known for many years and have an integral part in this story as well as those who have been involved more recently in the production of this volume. There are many of you and we didn't want to miss anyone so we aren't specifically mentioning your name here. You know who you are—Thank you and Godspeed.

We give special thanks to Rachel Mae Stutzman who conducted the initial interviews.

JOEL BUISSERETH

Introduction

As in a biographical sketch of this sort, "I" and "me" are used repeatedly. I have one request, dear reader, please don't let this detract from glory that belongs only to God. I am what I am, I have what I have, only by God's grace. All praise shall be to Him.

JOEL BUISSERETH

Map of Haiti

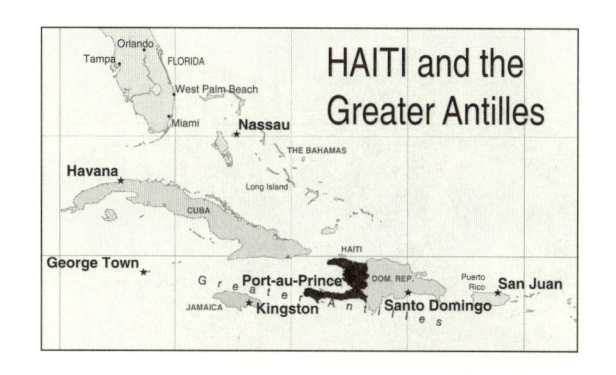

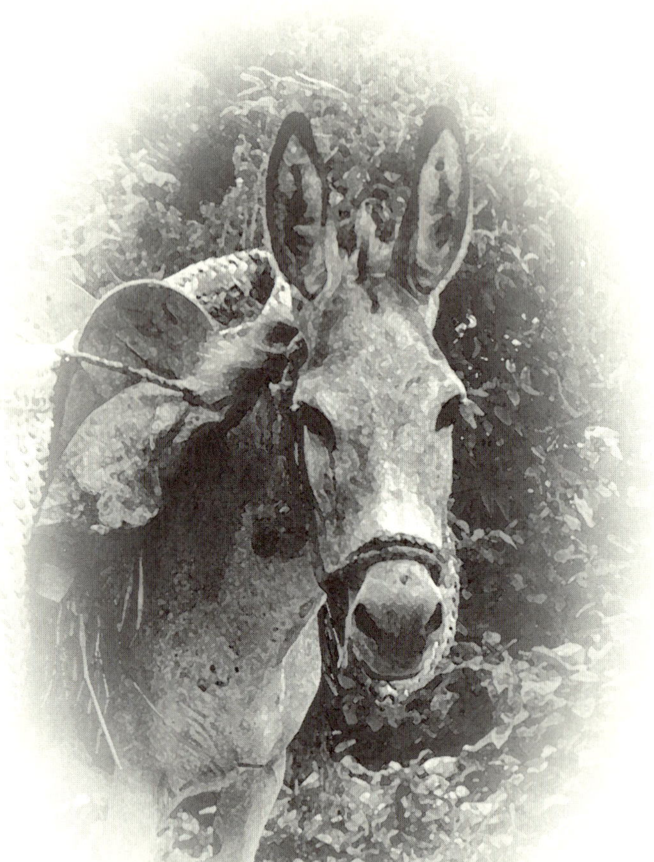

1

Hurricane Flora

Outside in the seemingly endless night, the fierce, relentlessly howling wind threatened to snatch the door from my grip. The men were taking turns holding the front door shut. I took my turn after my father—using all my strength to hang on to the metal hook on the inside of the wooden-plank door.

It was a tense, sleepless night in the remote village of Labaleine, Haiti. Our tiny thatched-roof hut was filled with frightened people whose homes had been blasted away by this ferocious storm. I was terrified.

It was around 7 PM, when the winds began to blow on the evening of October 3, 1963. Slowly chunks of thatch, branches, and twigs began flying around. We didn't know what was coming. Mother hurried with her cooking as the wind challenged her fire. Some neighbors nervously predicted, "Cyclone, cyclone."

We brought our two donkey jacks, one cow, several goats, and a few pigs in from the fields to safety. We tied the jacks, cow, and pigs in our yard and the goats in the *depot,* or storage building. A few neighbors took their animals inside their homes for protection. After we had the animals safe, we hurriedly ground millet grain with our wooden mortar and pestle inside Mother's cooking shack, so she would have something to cook during the storm. We gathered in the drying corn hanging on a *liane* vine from the palm tree in our yard.

During the night, devastating winds and rain crushed all the homes in the village of Labaleine except seven. When a house toppled, occupants would scurry to the nearest house still standing. More than sixty people were packed in our small two-room hut. We sang and prayed and sang and prayed all night long. Fear gripped our hearts. Singing and praying were our only hope. Father led the prayers and everyone joined audibly. Our clothes were wet. Our spirits were dampened. And we were cold.

I was 12 years old when Hurricane Flora swept across southern Haiti, and its havoc would impact the country for years to come. The pleasantness of my childhood was history. Everything from our mud-plastered-wood dwellings to the economic and social infrastructures of Haiti's panhandle was upended—literally overnight. The Haitian people are still trying to recover from that blast of 1963.

During the evening and through the night, young neighborhood men were out in the storm, going from house to house, checking to see that everyone was safe. When the wind increased, they took shelter in the closest house before they resumed their mission. The men carried some of the children and older people to safety in one of the remaining houses.

If not for the courageous efforts of these men, one of the villagers, Despe, would surely have died. Afraid that his house would fall, he had sought refuge in Divermo's house. Both men ended up being covered with debris when Divermo's house collapsed. When the village men came searching, Despe responded. He had a bruise on his head that he probably had gotten from a beam when it came crashing down. He was pinned and needed help to get free. Despe survived with a scar on his head. Divermo also was injured.

Lenes and his 5- or 6-year-old son, Lebones, were found dead under the crushed remains of their house. Also killed was Planye, who lived alone. His body was found under the wreckage of his house.

Our three coconut trees and all our mango trees close to the house toppled, but, praise to God, we still had our house. Some of the houses that toppled were built stronger than ours. Under normal conditions thatched roofs in our area can last up to 50 years, but a hurricane is not a normal condition.

The people who stayed at our house returned to their damaged houses the next morning and brought back clothes and household items they were able to salvage, and stored them inside our house. The next few days some of the cooks of the refugee families built fires in various spots in our yard to do their cooking. Mother and a few other ladies built fires under the roof of our dirt-floor porch. Starting a fire was a challenge using wet twigs on the wet ground.

Many goats, donkeys, and pigs were killed by the hurricane. The following day some of the dead animals were cut up and the meat was put in brine to preserve it.

In addition to all this activity, Mother and another lady who boarded at our house each gave birth to a baby girl the week after the hurricane. October 10 was the day my sister Esther was born. Coincidentally, the village midwife was also staying at our house and was able to help out.

More than sixty people packed into our house that first night. Some of them stayed at our house for three months. Evenings were spent singing and talking. I thought it was fun to have all those people in our house. After having been struck with fear by the hurricane, I felt a security in the presence of friends and neighbors.

The only time I wished the people were not at our house was at mealtime, when I got less food because we had to share with more people. My parents were glad to provide shelter and protection for our neighbors. They never talked about wishing it was otherwise.

After the hurricane, when I saw clouds overhead, I feared more hurricane weather was imminent. Even our parents were affected—for several months they didn't want us to wander too far from home, for fear that another hurricane would occur.

# 2

And After

The return to normal life was difficult. The rebuilding of homes and the reclamation of the land were hard. Seeing the effect on the land was a continual reminder that life was not the same anymore.

Many of the families built small, temporary structures near where their houses had stood, using leftover pieces. We called the small structures "tents." They were low A-frames made with poles and covered with thatch. The backs were closed and the fronts had openings big enough to pass through. They certainly were not very durable, but they provided protection for the people's possessions and a place to sleep.

The storm came at the end of avocado season, and many avocado branches were blown to the ground. We had fun going out and picking up the delicious fruit. This was a treat because in normal times we were not allowed to go into another's field and pick up fruit without permission from the owner.

One discomfort after the hurricane was the presence of blood-sucking body lice in our hair and shirt collars. It was very embarrassing to have lice because it implied that you were a dirty person. Usually people wouldn't confess to having lice, but since so many people had them, we found out.

Another blood-sucking bug that appeared after the hurricane, in addition to the lice, was the *pinèz* (bed bugs). We heard that the *pinèz* appeared as a result of a reaction between malaria powder spray and moisture in thatch roofs and caning on chairs. At night they would hide in your bed and chair. When you offered a guest a chair, it was sometimes humiliating when they would sting the guest.

At night, after we turned off our little kerosene lamp, the bed bugs would begin dropping from the hay in the roof onto our beds. I am convinced they smelled us. These were even worse than lice, because lice only came to you if you were dirty. *Pinèz* would come to anyone.

The hurricane downed mango trees by the hundreds. These trees provided excellent material to make charcoal. Before the hurricane, no one in Labaleine even knew how to make charcoal. Today, charcoal is the most lucrative cash income for the local men. Very few people in Labaleine use charcoal themselves. It is mostly sold to city people or dealers. After the hurricane charcoal became a means of survival as a cash income. A few of the men from Labaleine went to the nearby village of La Borieux to learn how to make it. Though charcoal is still a source of income, the resulting deforestation and the side effects of erosion and reduced rainfall pose a big problem for our country.

The charcoal of today is also of inferior quality comparatively. Formerly, only the hard Gaiac tree was used to make it. In the early 70s, after many years of cutting trees and not replanting, the demand outstripped the supply. Today, any kind of tree, soft or hard, is used because of the lack of Gaiac trees and the demand for charcoal. A handful of the high quality Gaiac charcoal might last up to a week, providing heat for two meals per day. After the food was cooked, the cook would dowse the embers and thus be able to use them again.

After the hurricane, neighbors helped us remake the footer of our house. The original footer had only posts placed in holes, with soil and rocks packed tightly around. For the new footer we dug a ditch all the way around the inside and outside edge of the house and underneath the walls and filled it with cement. We did it in sections so we would still be able to use our house. The bedroom walls were moved to make way for the reinforcement.

Fifty-pound bags of cement were hauled by mule and donkey, two bags per trip, over the five-mile stretch from the village of Fond-des-Blancs. With the help of friendly, willing neighbors—who compensate for limited resources in Haitian life—we hauled load after load of sand from the ocean to mix with the cement. We covered the floor of the front room with flat stones. The whole project took about a month, and helped close the unforgettable chapter of Hurricane Flora.

The Path of Faith

Because of the response from Christians in the States to the hurricane, the Lord allowed me to make important contacts that proved to be a vital part of my education and have changed my life forever.

A village hut

3
Childhood

My mother was always shy and reserved. The morning I was born, she had been sent by her parents to a field more than a quarter mile from home to retie some of their animals after they had been tied close to the house overnight. She began labor on the barren, hard-packed ground of her father's small livestock tying area. A nearby neighbor lady quickly carried the message to my grandmother, who came with a dress and wrapped me in it. It was April 15, 1951.

Mother and Father were both raised in Labaleine. Because of land availability, my father's father moved to Labaleine from Buissereth, the village named after my ancestors.

There were only two beds in our house at first—one for my parents and one for my brother Aurel and me. The bedposts and crosspieces were made of native mahogany wood. The bed was covered with a thick cornhusk or papyrus mat and bed sheets. The soft papyrus mat was made by tying together papyrus leaves, which are similar to coconut leaves. In later years we had another mat on the floor for the girls to sleep on. The most children at home was five. I was the oldest, followed by brother Aurel and sisters Clelie, Clement, and Esther. Later, after I left Labaleine to pursue my education, my youngest brother and sister, Jovin and Sonya, were born.

In my early teens when Aurel and I came home after dark and the door was locked, we would knock. Father would inquire from bed, "*Ki moun ki la?*" ("Who is there?"). Then he asked us where we had been and what we were doing. If he decided it was legitimate, he let us in. If not, he said we could sleep outside. We slept in our two-story, tin-roofed grain storage building or in the yard. At first it was a punishment to sleep outside, but soon we began to enjoy the freedom and independence. Eventually we slept outside regularly and the girls used our bed.

In the storage building we slept on piles of millet heads. After the millet was gone, we often slept on a bundle of scraped sisal that was ready to be tied into bales and sold.

One morning after spending the night in the storage building, I discovered that a rat had bitten my one big toe. I've heard that rats blow as they bite so you can't feel it. There's a Haitian proverb, *When some people want to get something from you, they are like a rat. They bite and blow so you won't feel the pain.*

We had two meals a day. Our breakfast was coffee and bread. Sometimes I had *manyòk,* a root crop that is about 12 inches long and is grated, pressed, and cooked. At times I also had *tablet,* a

Childhood

*Our family's depot
and cooking shack*

snack made with sliced coconut and peanuts that looks just like American peanut brittle. The main course, served in the evening, was often corn mush or millet and beans. Mother would crack the grains of the foxtail-like millet heads or shelled corn by stamping it in our mortar and pestle. After the millet or corn was cracked, Mother would winnow it by tossing it slightly in the air from a round tray.

There was a lady who bought and slaughtered pigs and sold their meat and lard. We rarely had meat dishes at home, except when we had visitors or for other special occasions such as our Independence Day on January 1 or weddings. However, Mother often put diced pork into our *sòs pwa,* or sauce beans. Most of our meat was purchased at the market or from the local butcher lady. Usually animals were taken to market and bought by slaughterhouses. Not many people in Labaleine slaughtered and processed their own livestock, except for goats and chickens for special occasions, or if an animal was strangled. Not everyone had a donkey, but every family had at least one goat, one pig, and some chickens. Nearly every family had at least one cow.

Chickens ran loose in the yard around our house. We kept them for their meat that we enjoyed on special occasions. The chickens would clean up leftover millet grains around the yard and in the field and laid lots of eggs. It was rare that we used the eggs. Most of the time we just let the chickens nest. We preferred having more chickens to eating the eggs. Having a large flock of chickens was considered prestigious.

Childhood

Outside our house we had a grinder that the neighbors used. In return, they left a cup of cornmeal for us and the chaff to feed to our pigs.

Even though I never experienced starvation firsthand, I would say I grew up in poor conditions. Of course, as children, we would have enjoyed more food.

During the day we enjoyed avocadoes, mangoes, *sapoti*, *zabriko*, sweet oranges, and grapefruits off our own land. Sometimes when we were working in the field, we built a fire and roasted corn or cooked sweet potatoes.

At mealtime, Father was the only one to eat at the table. We children got our food at the table and ate outside or on a chair in the same room. We never dared to eat at the table with Father; this would be much too disrespectful.

Mother ate her portion in the shack beside the house where she did her cooking. In all my years at home, I never saw my father and mother eat together. I believe this style of mealtime came from the slave era, when the master ate at the table and the servants ate elsewhere. Even though I grew up with this, I don't endorse this concept. We can see in Scripture that Jesus ate with His disciples, which implies it is not a matter of disrespect.

As I was growing up, I felt the urge in my heart to change this in my own family. After I was married and we had children, we ate together as a family, even after we moved back to Haiti in 1993.

In our culture it is not good manners for a man to sit next to the fire while his wife is cooking. In Creole we would say that such a man is *ava*—too impatient! The only time that a fireside squat by the man is permissible is if he does it to keep warm.

Playing with neighbor children, we built dirt houses and played church, imitating our parents. We also spun wooden tops and flew our homemade kites. Sometimes when Father gave me money to buy candy or other food at the school, I would save some of the money to spend on kite material or tops.

I made my kites with coconut stems that I bent and tied together with my own homemade sisal string, and covered them with used sheets of paper from school. The sheets of paper had to be used ones, not blanks. Using blanks was an offense sometimes worthy of a spanking. Father didn't allow a big kite because we would have had to buy brown paper-bag material at the market to cover it. Enough material for one kite may have cost from 30 to 50¢ (Htn.), and that was too much. We used *candelabra* milk from the *candelab,* a cactus plant, or *amidon,* a liquid from the *manyòk* plant, to glue them together. I straddled a separate piece of paper over the crosspiece that would make a loud noise when the wind passed through.

My friends' kites were more elaborate. Some would add a tail to their kite and hang razor blades on it. The razors would cut the strings of other kites while in the air. Limited resources certainly encourage creativity!

Even though no work was expected from us during the day on

Childhood

Saturday and on Sunday afternoon, there was still some restraint from my parents about playing. We always found ways to get out and play secretively though. I would often sneak out to go kite flying on Sunday afternoon. Though I enjoyed being with friends, my father didn't like the gang atmosphere and negative influence other children might have on me.

We played telephone with white string attached to empty cardboard *digo* boxes at each end. *Digo* was a dye Mother used if she wanted to add a slight tint to white clothing. I don't know where the telephone idea originated because we had never even seen a telephone. We also played speculator, trying to sell sisal scraps to our friends. Our pretended weighing apparatus was a sisal rope dangling from a tree. It never did work too well.

Father was strict, and if I was discovered playing while I should have been working, he would whip me. He wouldn't use his hand because he said he didn't want to hurt himself. He wanted to hurt us. He said he would never use a branch that was straight and clean—always one with four or five little twigs on the end to make sure it hurt. Only later did I realize that the strictness at home was for my benefit.

Our parents didn't want us to play dominoes like many of the other children because that was associated with gambling. To fill some of the need for excitement and activity, about ten of us neighbor children often went from house to house in the community to sing, pray, and recite Bible verses in the evening.

The Path of Faith

In my early teens I made my own guitar. I made it from a used oil can and thin wire strings. I often got it out in the evenings and just strummed around on it. Even though I couldn't play songs on it, I still enjoyed strumming while I hummed or sang.

One morning my father sent me to one of our fields to gather sour oranges to feed the pigs. (Pigs were fed sour oranges, suckers from the cacti sisal plant, and palm tree seeds.)

Sour oranges are so acidic that the juice sizzles when you squeeze it onto the ground, but the pigs loved them. I was supposed to fill the two saddlebags on my donkey. After I left the house, I met a young fellow whom I knew was on the way to the same area, because his parents owned land there. The boy was known to be a troublemaker. He suggested we go together since we were going to the same place. I consented, thinking he could help me pick the oranges. Within a short distance were a few coconut trees. He climbed one of the trees and started dropping coconuts. We enjoyed the coconuts together. The coconut trees didn't belong to anyone. Next we got distracted by throwing stones at birds. He asked me to go with him to his parents' field and suggested we could get my oranges on our way back. It sounded like a good idea because that way he could help me. But we got distracted chewing sugarcane and looking for birds' nests.

The boy was probably thirteen and I was about eight. We spent all the time joking and playing. I was in a hurry to get back, and we didn't take time to fill my two saddlebags like Father had asked

Childhood

me. I should have returned in about 2 hours. Instead it was about 3½ hours before we even started back. Over halfway home I heard someone calling me. No one but my father! When the other fellow saw my father, he took off running. I continued with my donkey and walked into my fate. A hefty whipping was my order. I know the other fellow would have felt the pain too if he would have stayed.

The boy later moved to northern Haiti, where he allegedly stole and ate poisoned food. Later his body became peppered with sores, and he was quarantined in his mother's cooking and food storage shack in Labaleine, where his parents cared for him. Worms infested the sores and he eventually died.

While this unfortunate young man was growing up, his parents were not very firm with their discipline. This was a lesson for me on the importance of being respectful to my parents, and I gained a new appreciation for my father's strictness. I believe Father saw the big picture and was preparing me for the future.

Father was concerned for us children, that we would not be lazy. He wanted us to be like the ant, which has no leader yet stores up for the winter. He wanted us to be working. Father didn't have a big problem if I was with friends who were respectful and obedient. Joking, talking, and socializing were okay in the evening, but during the day he expected us to be working.

I remember the fathers of some of us boys threatening to send us to Maison Centrale, a rigid youth camp in Carrefour, a suburb of Port-au-Prince. We actually wished among ourselves that we could go and learn how to be a mechanic or a truck driver or a pilot. We wished our parents were serious. This would have meant we could go to Port-au-Prince, and going to Port is everyone's aspiration.

My sister Cleante was born in 1965. When Cleante was 3 months old, she became sick. Father got medication and was directed to give it with a teaspoon, but in the countryside a spoon is a spoon. Instead of a teaspoon a tablespoon was used. Little Cleante only lived for a few days. I remember how her small wooden casket fascinated me.

The medication for Cleante probably came from Dr. Momple of Fond-des-Negres. Later someone who was at our house read the label. It directed that a small spoon needs to be used when it is given to children. A small spoon? We didn't have a small spoon. That's when we realized little Cleante probably died from an overdose of medicine.

I don't think Dr. Momple was a licensed doctor, but he gave shots to sick people. My uncle Albert told me that Dr. Momple didn't treat people in a traditional way. He probably employed some divination practices. He would always carry medicine in his briefcase. Some Haitians are slow to seek medical help when they are sick. Usually they wait to see if it will heal by itself. While I was growing up, there was no doctor or nurse in our immediate village, and Dr. Momple was a good three hours away by mule.

Childhood

Sharing is a way of life in Haitian communities. Our people live close together, and the neighbors know when someone doesn't have enough food. Sharing immediately goes into effect. Actually, in Haiti neighbors are always sharing. The spirit of goodwill is an integral part of my culture. Mother would prepare a few plates and share with the neighbors every evening, whether they had a need for food or not. She often got a gift in return. After the plate was empty, the recipient would wash the plate and return it to the sender with a verbal "thank you." A note could not be sent because most people were illiterate. One of us children would always return the gift plates. After we were grown, Mother had neighbor children deliver and return her plates.

The food was usually shared with the same people, and it wasn't much. According to the Haitian proverb, *Giving a little does not mean that you are stingy.*

South of the mission compound toward La Borieux are acres and acres of land. Any person in Labaleine who didn't own or sharecrop land in this area was considered lazy.

Father once asked me to do something in our field there. I don't remember what it was. I do remember that I got distracted, thanks to my friend Ronezi, now married to my sister Clelie. Ronezi and some other young boys persuaded me to go with them to see the ocean. Of course I was interested to go to the ocean, because I hardly ever went there. We had heard talk about the *kayiman,* a tropical American crocodile, that could be life threatening. We were too curious and adventurous to pass it up.

A fisherman from La Borieux had a large catch of fish in his net, and other men were helping him get it to shore. The man was nervously bobbing up and down in his canoe, worrying that he would lose his catch. When we arrived, he summoned our help, and we ran to the rescue and were able to land the catch. It was the biggest pile of fish I had ever seen.

We proudly walked away, each with a two-hand clasp of fish that he'd given us in appreciation for our help. Since I wouldn't be allowed to take my fish home, we built a fire in a nearby field owned by the father of one of my friends who was with us. We ate every last fish.

It was mid-afternoon when we started toward home, and Father had asked me to be home by noon. On our way back I spotted my father coming in our direction. My pride went down the drain.

As we neared, I saw that he had his hands behind his back. I knew immediately he must have a whip in his hand. I told Ronezi that I'm getting a whipping because I had spent too much time away. Ronezi had been walking beside me, but at that point he started walking ahead of me. When we met Father, Ronezi, who is about 6 or 7 years older than me, told Father that I was with him and assured him that it was okay. My father had a lot of respect for Ronezi's parents. Would you believe it? My dear friend Ronezi spared me of a whipping.

Childhood

The first thing I did every morning was to wash my face with water I poured from a gourd into an enameled cup. A rule in our culture is that you shouldn't say *Bonjou* ("Good Morning") to anyone before washing your face. I would also slide my finger across my teeth to clean them, since I had no toothbrush. I didn't have a toothbrush until I was in my mid-teens.

Sleeping-in was not an option in our family. Sleeping too much was what lazy people did, and Father didn't want lazy children. There is a Haitian proverb that my father liked and repeated often. *If you sleep too much, your blood will turn to water.*

If we were awake and wanted to snooze, Father reminded us of the Proverb about the ant. Sometimes just to hear Father's voice is all it took to get us up. Mother was more lenient and would let us snooze.

The donkeys were tied in the field during the night so we could use them during the day. The goats in turn would graze during the day and would be near the house during the night. Retying the

> *Go to the ant, thou sluggard; consider her ways, and be wise: Which having no guide, overseer, or ruler, provideth her meat in the summer, and gathereth her food in the harvest.*
>
> Proverbs 6:6-8

animals was part of the daily chores for us children. Sometimes when we got to the site where the animals had been tied, they were nowhere to be seen. Fearing wasps and garter snakes, we stepped cautiously through the pasture, looking for footprints, droppings, or some other clue to track down our animals. Sometimes the rope stripped off the sapling where the animal had been tied. Sometimes the rope tore. It wasn't such a big deal if the animals were loose and stayed in the area, but if they went on someone else's property, it became an issue. Sometimes when we lost an animal, neighbors would tell my father, and he would come to the field to help us. Usually if Father came to check on us, he would dole out discipline.

One summer morning when I was bringing a mule from the field, I decided to have the mule drag me so I wouldn't have to walk. I hung onto the rope and leaned backwards with my calves nearly touching the ground. I whipped the mule and he ran up the hill. When I got to the plateau at the top, my foot hit a rock, and I lost my balance. I fell on a sharp little tree stump that jutted from the ground. It pierced my jawbone, and some pieces of wood remained embedded for several years thereafter. To kill the infection I put wood ashes on it, from a burned field nearby.

Brother Aurel cared for a neighbor's goat. In two years she had five little ones. There was a rule that if the animal had a female offspring, the caretaker got it. If a male, the owner kept it. Actually, if there was only one baby, the caretaker and owner of the mother split ownership, half and half. The next year when another baby came along, the caretaker and owner would each have one animal. I once cared for a neighbor's cow, but she never had offspring. I got paid with one-fourth of the sale price when she was sold.

When a child is born in Haiti, the parents choose a godfather and godmother. They are the replacement parents in case of a fatality. At my birth, Uncle Albert was named my godfather. When I was about one year old, he gave me a goat. Father gave it to a man in La Borieux, so he could care for it. Each fall before school started, Father and I had an enjoyable walk to the oceanside village of La Borieux, to give payment or make a deal on offspring from the previous year. If my goat had twins, we sold the one at the market, which helped Father pay for my school uniforms and books. The other was given to the caretaker as payment.

At the beginning of each year, sister Clelie would visit her godfather, who lived in our village. I would go with her and help carry her gifts of cola drink and bread. Until she was about 16 and moved to Miragoane he would always give Clelie two *gourdes*. At that time two *gourdes* would have been enough to buy two small goats. I was filled with jealousy by this great sum of money. She was younger than I, and it just didn't seem fair that she would get this large sum of money.

After a heavy rain, there was a stream behind our house where we would sometimes bathe a few times a day. We didn't use soap or a towel. We just waded in, splashed around, and dried in the sun.

Before we had wells in Labaleine, people depended on the springs for water. The main spring, located south of Labaleine, is still running. I once measured the output of the spring at 50 gallons per minute. People from the neighboring areas of Trompe and Kay Chalin also depended on this spring. After heavy rains, another spring in Kay Chalin, the next village to the northwest, would begin bubbling up from under a big *mapou* tree. While the water was at the surface, we got our water there; but after it dried up, we needed to go to the spring more than two miles down the path. I don't remember that there was ever a shortage of water.

Aurel and I were responsible to keep our family supplied with water. We could load ten gourds into the bags on our donkey. Sometimes we would arrange it so we could bring home a few gourds of water on the way back from working in the field during the day. Often we would also bring home dry sticks for Mother to use for cooking.

We raised the gourds on our own trees. One tree could have as many as 25 gourds or more. Those we didn't use for water containers were used for grain or salt storage in Mother's kitchen.

The donkey that hauled water got a drink about every day. Cows only got water about once every three or four days. We never took the goats to the spring for water; they got enough through vegetation.

One morning on my nearly two-mile trip back from the spring, my donkey lost its balance and fell to the ground, breaking three

Childhood

Chores

The Path of Faith

or four of the gourds. In those days the path was rugged and only about six feet wide. When I came home and my parents heard about the mishap, they blamed me for not being careful. Father switched me on my seat with a small branch. The gourds had to be replaced.

When we had gourds that needed to be repaired, we used tar from the *goudwon*, a fruit the size of an apple and shaped like a bell. We would poke a stick through the *goudwon* to hold it, then we held the bottom of the fruit into the fire to set it aflame, and held the leaking gourd beneath. The *goudwon* would begin dripping on the small holes in the gourd and seal them shut. The big holes needed to be filled with a piece of cloth or a small stick first, and the *goudwon* tar would then seal it. If there was only a crack, too small for paper, we would fill it with soap before sealing with tar. We also had 5- to 7-gallon metal containers from the market, but we used them mostly for cooking.

The first well in the village was drilled in 1967, south of the mission compound, in an effort to make water accessible to more people. It was coordinated by Nelson S. Miller of Sugarcreek, Ohio, and Paul Gingerich from Kalona, Iowa. Today there are six wells in the community.

I never, in all my life, experienced a dearth of clothing. I remember my first pair of dress shoes was brown. I only wore them on the first day of the year and on special occasions such as weddings. I had imported plastic sandals to go to church and school.

Childhood

My sandals to work in the field were made by a cobbler in Vieuxbourg, who would measure my feet and then custom-make the soles from rubber tires and the straps from rubber tubes. Everyone wore these to work in the field. Even today these are worn a lot.

Shoes that fit properly were sometimes hard to find. If we didn't find shoes in one village market, we would go to the next. We couldn't buy ready-made shirts or pants. We had tailor-made clothes. Even today, most people in Labaleine have their dress clothes tailor-made. We would go to market, buy our choice of fabric, and have the tailor custom-make our shirts and pants. A tailor couldn't afford to keep a stock of various sizes. His stock would need to be too large.

Even though ready-made clothes are available in Haiti, they are used clothes, probably from the U.S., and Haitians consider them inferior to tailor-made.

During U.S. President John F. Kennedy's reign in the 1960s, used clothes began coming to Haiti. The local people called them "Kennedy," thinking Kennedy sent them. Even today, used clothes—no matter where they come from—are dubbed "Kennedy" by the locals. Even though "Kennedy" clothes are worn for working, tailor-made are preferred for formal dress. Tailor-made are considered more durable. If someone gets a hole in a used garment, it's easily excused as "Kennedy." I didn't have ready-made, used clothing until missionaries began visiting our village and left them.

The Path of Faith

Tailors are in demand in Haiti. August is especially a busy time for tailoring, because this is when the school uniforms are sewn. Uniforms are used in all the schools across Haiti.

There was a tailor or seamstress in nearby Fond-des-Blancs, but father was a close friend to Joleme in La Colline, further west over the mountains, so we patronized him. When I started school, he charged 15¢ (Htn.) to sew pants and 10¢ (Htn.) for shirts.

There were always seamstresses in Labaleine, but in my culture it was less than dignified to have a lady sew for a man. For a young boy it was a lesser issue, but once you were in the teens or older, a man had to do the sewing for a man or boy. Seamstresses would sew for ladies. The same idea prevailed with haircuts for the men. Men would cut men's hair; I never saw otherwise.

Having pants patched by the ladies was okay, though. Actually, if a young girl patches pants and does a really good job and others hear about it, it reveals her ability as a seamstress, and puts her up for grabs.

Up to age 15, we were not allowed to wear long pants. Long pants signified maturity, which didn't go with childhood. I started wearing long pants at the beginning of the year I turned 16. We were considered one year older at the beginning of each year, no matter which month we were born. Father bought the fabric from a merchant at the Fond-des-Blancs market. I went along when Father bought the fabric so the merchant could measure me and determine the needed amount. I don't know when it changed, but short pants on young boys are no longer the standard.

When I was in my early teens, Father sent me to La Colline to pick up two short pants for my brother Aurel and me. Along the way I met a man headed in the opposite direction. The man gruffly asked where I was going. I told him I was going to the tailor Joleme. He further probed what I was going to do there. The man was very dark-skinned and evil looking.

I was scared by now. I told him I'm going to pick up two pairs of pants and buy some coffee for my parents. He demanded to see my money, and I pulled it from my pocket. He asked me to give it to him and return to my parents. I started back. He followed me for a short distance. Then he told me to wait, he wanted to talk to me. I was afraid he would kill me with the long machete he was carrying. He gave my money back. I was trembling with fear.

I continued on toward La Colline. When I arrived at the tailor's house, I told him of the encounter. He was shocked.

The tailor also sold coffee, and Father wanted one small *marmite* (equal to about one gallon). The cost was 50¢ (Htn.), but he only charged me 35¢ and gave me 15¢ back as a gift and an expression of sympathy.

On my way back I met the man again, walking along the narrow path. He asked to see the things I had bought and asked whether I had any money left. I told him I had none. He needed to see for himself and pinched around on the outside of my pants pocket but didn't feel the few coins that nestled at the bottom. When he left me, I didn't run, for fear he would follow me; but my feet became very light. When I came to the fork in the path, I took another route that was farther to home, but where people that I knew were working in their fields.

When I told the story to my parents and friends, they thought it sounded like a joke, because the man didn't take my money or do me any harm.

In the mid-1960s and 70s, the Service National for Eradication of Malaria (SNEM) sent men out to spray every house in the country with a disinfectant against malaria. An outbreak was probably expected after the hurricane.

Once a month men would come with an empty spray tank and powder, and the resident was responsible to provide the water. In 15-20 minutes both the inside and the outside of the house were sprayed.

On the day the sprayers were expected, we removed our furnishings. If the sprayers came to a house and no one was home and it was locked, they would still try to enter and spray without removing any furnishings. If someone would have protested, the community chief of police would have enforced compliance. If they would not have been able to enter, they would have reported it.

Another group passed out pills as an effort to stamp out malaria. Several men would come through with a census list seeking out everyone and giving pills. The list also showed our ages, and pills were given accordingly. They asked us to get water, then the pills were handed to us, and we needed to take them while they policingly watched. If people were out in the field, the men went to the field to give the pills. The pills seemed more effective than the spraying.

I expect these efforts were especially supported by our president, Francois Duvalier, because he had a doctorate degree and was perhaps a practicing doctor before he became president, hence his nickname, Papa Doc. His son, Jean-Claude, became president in 1971 at the age of 19. He was known as Baby Doc.

During this time, the main spring where the local people filled their gourds with water was also the drinking fountain for the livestock. After the gourds were filled, the animals would have their turn for a drink, and, of course, droppings were left near the water. Perhaps some of the malaria cases stemmed from this polluted water.

During the census of 1964, a group of men came to get a record of everyone in the community. As part of their record-keeping efforts, they gave every house a number. One man pumped the black paint and another sprayed number "51" on the top part of our doorframe.

Everyone has hot peppers planted at their house to use in their cooking. One time I was playing with one of Mother's peppers from a plant in front of our house, thinking it was not yet matured, and I happened to break the skin. My one eye itched at the same time, and I rubbed it. Soon both my eyes were burning so badly I couldn't open them. I ran up the mountain path behind our house to let them cool off. About 20 minutes later I was able to open my eyes again.

Once when I was riding a donkey down the mountain behind my mother's house, I made him gallop. All I had to steer him with was the rope wrapped around his nose and around his neck, and I hung to the other end of the rope. Just before I arrived at Uncle Jacque's house, I must have been going too fast when I went around the curve, because my donkey lost his balance. He landed on my left leg, with his feet uphill. I screamed for help, but nobody came. After I finally managed to get out, I flipped the donkey by ferris-wheeling his legs so he could get up.

My father had borrowed Manius' machete. On my way to return it, I pulled it from its sheath, pretending I was a man. I learned a hard lesson. I had the machete turned with the cutting side toward my hand and cut the webbing between my thumb and index finger. When I got home I put ashes on the cut, and mother wrapped it with cloth.

The machete is an essential element of life. It carries with it the sign of manhood. A man rarely leaves the house without it. Leaving for market, the machete goes into the bag.

When a boy is in his early 20s, he will buy a machete at the market. I left home at 18, so I never got mine, but I had a sickle. A machete had more masculine significance than a sickle.

My father kept his machete right inside the door on the wall. If Mother needed one, she used Father's old one that was kept in a corner in the front room of our house. Women and machetes, however, didn't quite blend.

In the 1960s, the chief of police from Fond-des-Blancs worked on improving the road from Route 44 to the road leading to Labaleine. At that time it didn't mean too much to me, but now it is wonderful. He organized the effort and required people to work every Saturday. He made it his own project. If the people didn't help, he gave them a detention, sending them to a Labaleine assistant where they probably served time at the assistant's house.

After Malodem became chief of police in our village, he continued the project. A few of the people who didn't want to cooperate got a detention. They went to Malodem's house and sat on a chair as their punishment. I helped a few times when Father was sick or unable to go. We used a pick, crowbar, or *rabot,* a long-handled plane.

In the years when the harvest was good, there was a greater abundance of food than there is today. I remember when my father took millet to market and wasn't able to sell it because of the surplus. He actually brought it back, cooked it, and fed it to the pigs. This was like dessert to the pigs, because livestock only got grain if there was extra. Otherwise they got the stalks from corn or other leftovers from our fields. In a drought year the animals only got vegetation they found on pasture. Our fields were used to raise food for our family and for cash crops. We never had a garden in our backyard, like Americans consider a garden.

Nowadays there don't seem to be surpluses. There are fewer farmers, and with all the erosion and faulty agriculture practices, the land doesn't produce as it used to. I believe the cost of living is high because of inflation and because the fields don't produce as they used to. There are also fewer people interested in agriculture. Through the Labaleine school we are hoping to raise up a host of new farmers who can read and write and will have the knowledge to implement new and better ways of farming.

I remember very vividly when there was a drought in 1968 and there were hardly any crops in the Labaleine area. We had to go as far as Miragoane, about 15 miles, to buy food. I don't know whether there was more rain in Miragoane or whether they shipped the food from La Gonave and Jeremie, 60 or 70 miles from Labaleine. (Jeremie is a prosperous town where lots of vegetables and coffee are grown.)

We ate lots of *cassava,* which is made from the *manyòk* plant. Normally we could depend on millet, but there was none that year. Mother also made dumplings and mixed them with bean sauce.

4

Kòvé

I enjoyed taking part in the *kòvé* (pronounced kaw' vay), when many local farmers worked together and traded labor. *Kòvé* is the Haitian way of helping one another—of friend helping friend overcome the challenges of daily life. Although *kòvé* is still practiced, it is not done as much now as when I was a boy. People are less interested, and because the land is less fruitful due to lack of rain and erosion, workers get discouraged.

Kòvé groups range from 10 to 80 men and boys. I joined when I was 16. The *kòvé* is active from Monday through Saturday. A person lends days to the *kòvé* in relation to what he thinks he needs to get the work done in his own field. Every farmer in the *kòvé* had one day when the *kòvé* group would work on his field. The following day the next person would get a day. Everyone took his turn. If you were part of a small group, *kòvé* would come to your field more often, but because of the smaller group less work would get done. With the larger groups, however, your turn would come less often, but more would get done.

The Path of Faith

Clearing the field, weeding, planting, or harvesting is the work that gets done by the *kòvé*. After the *kòvé* clears a farmer's field, it usually sits for a week to allow the residue to dry out before it is burned. The farmers believe it is good for the soil to clean off the residue by burning.

None of my father's fields were flat. Actually, tilling the level lowlands was more strenuous than the mountainside because there were more rocks. Our slanted fields also had rocks, but not as many as the lowlands. We pushed the rocks aside and planted among them.

During the summer I worked in *kòvé* every day. Often while we did the chores in the morning, Father organized the tools, sharpening machetes with a file and getting the sickles and picks ready to go. Aurel and I went to the pasture to get the donkeys and mules and returned to the house to load them up with the necessary tools for the work. The tools were put on the donkeys' backs on racks my father made of branches from hardwood trees. We tied the tools together and set them on top. The saddle blanket was a woven mat of *panno* grass that Father bought at the market.

Sometimes Father went to one farmer in the *kòvé* while Aurel and I went to another.

During the school year I would work in *kòvé* on Saturday. Singing while we worked made the day go faster. Someone would start singing, even if the workers were one hundred feet apart, and we all sang the same song. Many of the songs we sang were gospel songs, and even the men who were not Christians sang along. I can still picture the man who was planting as fast as he could and singing with all his heart, sweating profusely.

On schooldays, on my way home from school, I would always stop at the field where the men were working, especially when there was food involved.

The landowner's wife and other ladies cooked for the men in the *kòvé*. A normal day at *kòvé* went from 10 AM to about 4 PM. Sometimes the meal was served at 1 PM, and sometimes late afternoon, depending on the time of year. During the summer, when the days were longer, lunch was served at 1 PM because we would work until later in the day. During the short winter days, we ate before we left for home, between 3 and 5 PM.

After the ladies finished cooking the food in big kettles, they put banana leaves on top of the kettle and turned it upside down onto a tray on the ground. They then pulled the kettle away, leaving a big mound of corn mush or millet. Depending on the amount of people working, there would be four or five piles of food in a line. They would slice the mound with a big knife or a clean machete. A metal drum of about seven gallons was used to cook the bean sauce that was put in the bottom of the plate, with corn or millet on top. Some *kòvé* groups served alcohol, but my father's *kòvé* never did.

One summer when my father had a big *kòvé* and while lunch was being served, the men and boys could hardly eat because of the mosquitoes. They flocked around the men's mouths and ears.

Because we had just had an abundant rainfall, mosquitoes were out in force.

Rain meant mud. Often when trying to cross the creeks, our donkeys got stuck. None of the creeks in the Labaleine area have bridges. There is no need for bridges because the water is low enough that passage is usually no problem. In an ambitious effort funded by US/AID through the Pan American Development Foundation, 160 miles of roads in the area, including the Labaleine community, were rebuilt between 1995 and 1998. As a part of this project, the creek base was reinforced with rocks and concrete at various places where the road crosses.

My village name, Labaleine, means "the whale" in Creole, the practical language of Haiti. The mountains that border the valley form the shape of a whale. At one time a creek flowed down the middle of the whale. About halfway to the ocean a waterfall cascaded over an embankment. I enjoyed stopping there and throwing stones into the basin formed by the gushing water.

Many times in my boyhood days, with a greater abundance of rainfall, our donkey got hung up in the mud while hauling millet on the road that weaved in and out of the creek bed. Sometimes the road ran through the middle of the creek. Sometimes the road only crossed the water. In 1999, after 12 to14 hours of rain, the waterfall was flowing again. I hadn't seen it for a long time and witnessing that refreshed my spirit.

It was a great challenge during millet harvest, when we had a big load heading toward home, to get through the mud without getting stuck. We had to ease through, and even then we sometimes got stuck. We were happy when the water table was low, for travel at least. There was also an advantage in having an abundance of water while we worked in the field, because we could wash our feet and hands in the creek. People who owned land along the creek often planted the water-loving *mazonbel*, a yam-like vegetable. Sometimes I picked up stalks that the farmers had left beside the road. I enjoyed the taste of *mazonbel* and took them home for Mother to cook for us.

Konbit groups are similar to *kòvé*, but they are smaller and don't serve food. The men bring their own food. Farmers in the *konbit* work to the beat of drums. The *konbit* is also distinguished by the sound of the loud conch shell that one of the men blows a few times during the day.

Father didn't allow drums because they were often connected with evil spirits and Mardi Gras. When I was growing up, we had musical instruments in our church, but we never had drums.

The best thing about life in Labaleine before Hurricane Flora was the abundance of food and the low cost of living because we could raise most of our own food. The greatest challenge before Flora was the lack of education. Without education, the people weren't able to make wise decisions on their own. Land surveyors and lawyers were able to deceive the village people, and they didn't know the difference.

Poverty in Haiti is when one is unable to raise his own food, whereas poverty in America is lack of money. In Haiti, when I was growing up, if someone had plenty of food but didn't have money, it didn't affect that person too much. We didn't live off food that money bought, we lived from food that we raised in our fields. Of course, if we didn't have food, we would need to raise money to buy food. This is why the cost of living has increased today. What our people need, they sometimes need to buy, and it's more expensive than it was, too.

The Path of Faith

Sisal plant

5

Sisal

Every weekday a group of about 12 of us neighbors would go to the field and scrape sisal at 2:30 in the morning. Of course, it was nice when the moon was bright, but if it was dark, we scraped nonetheless. Even though this wasn't considered *kòvé,* we also exchanged labor. However, with sisal we took turns by the week. Each farmer in the group got a week at a time. On school days I left for school at 7 AM. During the summer, when we weren't going to school, we left for *kòvé* at about 10 AM. Often we would return to the field in the evening to beat more leaves in preparation for scraping the next morning. Usually we spent the night on-site, sleeping on dry, scraped sisal, donkey bags, or a mat that we took along.

Sisal is a large plant with tall erect leaves and looks similar to the aloe plant. Sisal plants grow to a height of 4 to 5 feet. Sisal leaves are prepared by beating them limp, one at a time, against a big rock. After the sisal leaf is beaten and scraped, the fibers are used to make twine, which is used in other countries for baling hay.

Sisal is also used to make rope that is sold within our own country.

After we finished scraping in the morning, we would spread the sisal in the sun to dry and cut more leaves for the next morning. Sticks from the tropical *bois d'orme* tree made the best scrapers. The *bois d'orme* is soft and lightweight, but when it is dry, it is hard to break. Since there was a shortage of these trees, we also scraped sisal with other wooden sticks wrapped with metal or with bamboo sticks.

My father would plant sisal in alternate sections so we could harvest year round. After a harvest was taken, we would need to wait three to four months before we could harvest again.

In addition to our own sisal crops, my father bought sisal from the neighbors. After an accumulation we would make the trip to one of the local villages to sell it. If we went to Miragoane, we rarely took a donkey because it was too far with the big loads. One or two of our uncles usually went with us.

Mules are bigger and can carry about 110 pounds on each side, while a donkey carries about half of that on a side.

When we traveled on Route 44 and a truck was stuck, the fellows would summon our help to fill the hole with rocks or help push the truck out. We willingly helped because that truck may someday be a lifesaver for us, too.

Trucks used to get stuck in the mud on the roads leading to Labaleine. After heavy rains, when water stood in the potholes, especially during the rainy season, big trucks often got stuck, and

Sisal

rocks were put underneath to provide traction to get out. Sometimes a truck would set for a week until enough mud was removed and the truck was able to get out.

Donkeys and mules were not exempt from getting hung up in mud. Usually we would lift the weight from the beast's back and urge it forward. The most dreaded procedure was when we had to untie the bales of sisal and set them off on the side. Then we would push at the animal to set it free.

We went to L' homond or Miragoane to sell our sisal, wherever the price was the best. We always traveled together with others from the community, each with their sisal bales on the back of a few mules or donkeys.

One time while I was beating sisal leaves, a needle at the end of one of the leaves poked me beside my kneecap. My father took a piece of cotton, from the cotton our family raised, and soaked it with castor oil. He put a thin layer on the puncture and lit it with fire from our kerosene lamp. Then he wrapped a cloth around my leg while it was still burning.

Many people raised cotton at the edge of their corn or millet fields. After we harvested our cotton, we hauled it to Aquin to have it run through a cotton gin. Later, if there was a need for it, we had a local mattress-maker come and stitch a four- to five-inch-thick mattress.

Other small crops we planted at the edge of the corn or millet were castor beans and pumpkins. Castor oil was made by roasting castor beans, then chopping them. Then we added water, cooked it, and drained the oil.

Pumpkin is used as a base for a delicious soup made with cabbage, potatoes, and other vegetables. The soup is served on January 1, the day we celebrate our independence from France in 1804.

6

The Gospel Comes to Labaleine

The gospel came to our village in 1937, after a group of people from Labaleine went to work in Nan Cloret, a small village north of Fond-des-Blancs. The village people from the Church of God in Christ presented the gospel, and a few Labaleine people were converted to faith in Jesus Christ. This small nucleus of believers came back and began meeting in a *tonnel,* a wooden-post structure covered with coconut leaves, in the village and began winning others to the faith.

Uncle Albert filled me in on this history. The Christians were treated as outcasts. Even though the Christians were invited to community activities, they didn't feel welcome. When the men who were Christians worked in *kòvé* or met at other social events, no one wanted to drink from their cups, and no one wanted to sit beside them. I believe the respect for the Christians began growing when the Christians would pray for the unbelievers when they were sick and were healed.

The Path of Faith

Today, more than 60 percent of the people in Labaleine, excluding the villages of Trompe and Kay Chalin, are committed Christians. I praise the Lord for my rich faith heritage. My village had about 14 years of solid Christian teaching before I was born. I thank God for laying a strong foundation where He later called me to build upon.

The first church building had mud-plastered walls with a wooden frame and a thatched roof. Later the church people smoothed the floor with lime and flat rocks and replaced the thatch on the roof with tin. This building was destroyed by the hurricane. For a few months after Flora, the church met at various homes, but usually at our home since Father was the pastor. After things were coming back to normal, we built a *tonnel* to meet in.

Our church was affiliated with the Church of God in Christ, but after the hurricane no one returned to help us. In 1964, the year after the hurricane, Father heard through Nestor, a friend of my father, of the Mennonites who were rebuilding houses in Côtes-de-Fer, 12 miles away.

Though Mennonite Disaster Service volunteers were asked to rebuild houses and not evangelize, a few took a serious interest in church planting. Two of these men were Aden Yoder of Sarasota, Florida, and Glen Martin of Dalton, Ohio. Pastor Tessier Ducasse from Miragoane translated for the MDS group and met with a returning group of Mennonites in April 1965, including Aden and Glen, to form *Mission Union Chretienne* (Christian Fellowship Mission, Inc.).

The Gospel Comes to Labaleine

Pastor Ducasse would later become an important link to help me fulfill my educational aspirations.

Nestor, who was a pastor and health agent from Fond-des-Blancs and knew my father and Pastor Ducasse very well, brought the two together. I think Father, Pastor Ducasse, and Nestor met in Fond-des-Blancs to discuss a plan for helping our church in Labaleine. This would have been Father's first encounter with the Mennonites.

I believe it was in 1966 when the Mennonites purchased a house and a plot of land near Miragoane and built a church building for Pastor Ducasse.

I remember taking charcoal and church activity reports to Pastor Ducasse's house. Since my father couldn't read or write, he told me the information for our church report and I wrote it down.

I still cherish the memory of the Sunday of my baptism in January 1966. I was 15 and enjoyed my involvement in the church with my father and looked forward to being more involved. Pastor Ducasse and two American couples visited. Lester and Darla Yancey from Sarasota, Florida, and Glen and Betty Martin from Dalton, Ohio, were the first American missionaries I had ever seen. The children in the village were especially intrigued by the *blancs*, the white people. I was overjoyed that they came on the day of my baptism.

After a short meeting at the church, everyone walked to the river about two miles away. Brother Christian Eliassaint from Pastor

The Path of Faith

Ducasse's church in Miragoane led the singing and played an accordion as we walked.

I could still point to the place where I was led into the water, dressed in a white robe, to meet Pastor Ducasse and Pastor Prosper, our district pastor, for my baptismal ceremony. Father observed from the water's edge, and the church people were singing behind him. I was baptized along with three ladies from our church.

We returned to our small arbor church for communion services. Betty Martin didn't know what to do about taking the communion cup. She couldn't stand the idea of drinking from the same cup as everyone else, even though the pastor wiped it with a napkin after each person partook. She felt humbled and emotional when the pastor brought the cup to her first.

After services, the guests met at the home of our deacon, Julne Celestin, for lunch. I remember that Darla and Betty made popcorn for us—the first real popcorn I had ever seen. The popcorn I knew was the corn we raised in the field and roasted in a kettle. We called our corn "popcorn," but only about half the kernels would pop.

While my father worked under Pastor Ducasse, he occasionally got word that food was available from the mission headquarters. Father would bring it home and make sure that everyone in the community got a share of it. When he would see the member of a family, he would tell them to send their children with a bag, and he would give them a portion. I made a list in Father's notebook of all the families in the community. Father doled out the food, and I made a checkmark by the family's name.

Working with my father inspired me to live a life of helping others. However, to me it is sad to see situations where people are lined up and food given to those who would be able to work.

Today, when food is received at the mission in Labaleine, we put the food to work. We still make sure that everyone gets some, but we arrange it that they work on the road to earn it. We divide into work groups of 20. The groups can work one day or one week, depending on the quantity of food available.

In 1967, Mission Union Chretienne bought a plot west of the current mission compound, and Lester Yancey from Florida brought a group of Mennonite men to frame the church building. Materials were sent from MUC via truck to Fond-des-Blancs. From there community people—churchgoers or not—carried the materials on their shoulders or on their donkey or mule to an outbuilding at one of the church people's homes in Labaleine.

Another thing I remember is that Desius and I walked to the spring about a mile away to get water. I was very tired from the intensity of the work, and I nearly fell asleep while we were walking down the path.

I was 16 when Lester Yancey's crew built the church building. I helped break stones for gravel for use in the concrete. I collected rocks around the building site, and I still remember Lester saying, "Small man, small rocks; big man, big rocks."

The Path of Faith

The finish work was done by the locals.

In 1979, while I was in the States, my father, with the help of Willis Miller of Kalona, Iowa, built the church building inside the mission compound at the spot of the village's first church building. We used it until it was replaced in the summer of 2000. Initial funds for the new church building were contributed by the Souderton Mennonite Church from Pennsylvania. We knew Willis through his involvement in the Miragoane mission in the early 1970s. His son, Leon, and wife, Joy, had also spent time in Miragoane as VSers.

When I was about 18 or 19 years old, I went with people from our church on a missionary journey. We started in Labaleine and traveled all the way to Miragoane. We traveled on foot—men, women, and youth. We stopped mostly at churches to preach the gospel, but we also stopped at houses to pray. When we returned home, we had a special prayer service at our house. As I recall, while we were singing *Holy God, We Praise Thy Name*, I closed my eyes and in my spirit I was up in the air and heard the others singing below loud and clear. I didn't see anyone, but I heard the singing. I shed lots of tears as I sang. At the end of the song—in spirit, I was back in our house.

About 15 of us walked for about two weeks. The man who instigated it prayed for the sick and dealt with the demon-possessed. Sometimes he claimed it was revealed to him that there were things buried in a given person's yard that the witch doctor had put there as a curse. Much fasting and praying was going on in the community. Some were speaking in tongues. I heard them speak words I didn't understand.

The group was all recruited as volunteers. He would also have fasting services periodically. People would often congregate from about 8 PM until dawn to pray. Sometimes the fasting services were held during the day. During these services no food was served.

The Path of Faith

Haitian lamp

7

School

I was about six when I began attending the local home school with about twelve others at the house of our tutor, Rodies. Other students who attended the formal school near Fond-des-Blancs joined us at Rodies' house during the summer, putting the count to about twenty students.

Rodies didn't allow his students to point with their finger while reading; he thought the finger was too big. My parents couldn't afford for me to have a pencil at the school, so I picked up the straightest and smoothest stick I could find along the path. To make it smoother I used one of my father's old shaving razors. Even though I had a pencil at home, my parents couldn't afford to let me take it to school. Rodies would write the date at the top of the paper and would make the first letter for us to pattern after for a writing homework assignment.

I remember my first writing exercise was to make about ten slanted lines. The next was a continuous lowercase cursive "L" design. Many times in a school day, Rodies would encourage us by saying, "Do it slow and do it well." I learned to identify letters under his tutelage.

I doubt that Rodies ever attended a formal school. He probably learned how to read and count from tutors as well.

Repetition was an underlying concept in those early days of my education with Rodies. Now, years later, I still remember some of the poems we learned.

People who visited our village and were connected with the church or school usually stayed at our house. Over the years many people lodged at our home because of Father's leadership in the church. Emond Prosper from La Colline stayed at our house during the two years that he taught at the school. I remember one morning my belt was broken, and he gave me the only one he had, which I used until Father bought me another one. While he was staying at our home, he taught my brother Aurel how to read, since he had difficulty learning in school. Aurel was more farming-oriented than I was.

While I was growing up, children didn't begin attending school until they were nine or ten years old. This meant children would be somewhat behind schedule all through their school years. The condition of the schools and education in this respect was less than ideal. Children began late because parents were concerned for the safety of their children walking long distances at a young age, and also because of the need for the children's help in the fields to provide food for the family. For a child to sit in school all day without doing manual labor was a foreign concept, and some families couldn't spare the time and money. Lack of resources was also a factor.

Some parents criticized others for sending their children to school. I longed to be able to go to school, and because of my passion my parents sometimes threatened to keep me out of school when I disobeyed. Some of my friends were kept from school, and today some of them cannot even write their own names. Today, parents are seeing the value of sending their children to school at a younger age. The educational landscape has changed tremendously. In our area where there was one school in the 1960s, there are about two dozen today. There is a proverb in our culture: *If you support your children when they are young, when they become older they will find you a bone to chew on.*

In Psalm 1, the Bible says that the person who doesn't walk in the counsel of the ungodly is like a tree planted by the water. The next expression says that he produces fruit every season, and producing every season means a lot of fruit. To be able to harvest every season you have to plant every season.

Regardless what it takes to encourage the young people to equip themselves in this season and equip themselves in the next season and the next, I feel we need to do it. It's like a farmer who plants corn every month. His harvest will be in cycles. If we don't work on these different cycles, one cycle will be lost somewhere in the cracks. And each cycle represents a generation.

When a community is excluded from the educational program, it will lose its identity. Uneducated people are likely to be less trusting and believing and often fall into superstition as a result.

My parents had no formal education. Neither of my parents could so much as write their name. They made an "X" when asked for a signature. In my parents' generation, people near cities such as Aquin and Port-au-Prince had easier access to schools and got an education, but smaller villages were deprived.

Uncle Albert, who is about 70 years old, knows so many stories that I can't remember them all. My poor uncle can't read; he can't even write his name. He is a very good listener but has had no formal education. It is sad that all those generations have been wasted.

Lexines Maignan, the oldest teacher at the Labaleine school and the one who helped my father start the school, forced himself to attend school at Fond-des-Blancs. His parents didn't want him to go, but he was able to go to about the 7th grade. He's a genius in math and even designed and built his own house.

Today, with the school we have in Labaleine, we basically crusade around the community, and if anyone has children who are not going to school, we want to know why. We act as academic policemen. During enrollment in January, teachers go to homes where students are not being sent to school to find out why. We want to eradicate and eliminate illiteracy.

School

There are people who have lived in Labaleine for a long time who have a lot of potential. There is a saying from the United Negro College Fund—*A mind is a terrible thing to waste*. Many minds have been wasted in Labaleine. The people were able to raise cows and goats, buy land and raise food, but that's about it. When it came to schooling and literacy, they threw it away. Now, though, illiteracy has been stopped, and we trust that it will be stopped forever, until Christ returns.

Despite difficult times the Lord opened the eyes of my parents to see the value of education. In 1959 I began at the school in Gaspard near Fond-des-Blancs at the age of 8. Usually I walked alone up the seven-mile *dèmòn* (meaning beyond the mountain) path behind our house.

Ferme Ecole de Fond-des-Blancs was arranged in three buildings. Infantine 2 and Preparatory 1 and 2, same as grades 1 to 3 in the U.S., were in Building A. Building B had Elementary 1 and 2, same as grades 4 and 5. Building C housed Intermediate 1, equivalent to grade 6; and Intermediate 2, like grade 7, was held outside under a mango tree.

Father wanted me to go to school, but it was so far away; and because I was the oldest child, he needed my help in the field. In addition to the $1 (Htn.) per year for tuition, we had the expense of buying our own uniforms, shoes, notebooks, pencils, and books. To be able to walk seven miles and be able to concentrate and study, I usually had a warm breakfast of millet, corn mush, or coffee and bread, and was given three or four cents (Htn.) to buy lunch at the school. One cent would buy a four-inch *tablet* or 10 mangoes. I also ate mangoes from along the *dèmòn* path along the way. Fruits hanging over the path were free.

The government charged sales tax when something was sold at the market. Tolls were charged on roads out of bigger villages, and I expect these revenues helped keep the schools going.

The Fond-des-Blancs school was pressed for space. There were not enough benches for all the students. Some sat on tops of desks and some on the windowsills of the one-and-one-half-foot poured-concrete walls. The remaining students sat on the concrete floor. The next nearest school was in Flamand, about 10 miles away.

There was no canteen or water on the school grounds. If we wanted water, we went to homes near the school. There was a restroom there, but it was in very poor condition.

Though many things about the Fond-des-Blancs school were less than ideal, any willing student was still able to get a good education.

Because of the many students at the school, the school administration didn't find out when I arrived the first day. On my own I chose to attend in Building B, thinking I was at that level and because I knew other Labaleine students who attended in that building. I was the only one from Labaleine who started that year. Some of the students in my class who came from other areas made it hard for me on my first day. Students that sat close knuckled me

School

on my head and came from the back and pulled my ears and pinched my skin because I was a newcomer. After the first day some of my friends from Labaleine who were in my class suggested I go to Building A to where the students were younger and start from the bottom. The next day I went to Building A in Preparatory 1, equivalent to first grade in the States. The education I received through Rodies and other tutors could be considered a very basic first grade. I learned to identify letters but was not able to read. The teacher in Building A asked where I came from. This is when they first discovered my presence.

On the way to school I would often see other students at the top of two different mountaintops, and then we would race to see who could get to the crossing of the paths near the school first. Sometimes when I didn't see any students, I asked people at the homes along the way if they had seen anyone go by. If they said yes, I knew I was late and had to run. If no, I was relieved. I just went by the sun to tell the time because I had no watch. Actually we didn't have a clock at home. We watched the sun during the day and the stars by night to tell the time. We also depended on the number of rooster crows during the night to help us determine the time.

On the way home from school, when I hung around with other students, we fought many wrestling matches. My cousin Ednor was the chief—no one could put his back to the sod.

Even though the Haitian government provided local schools, there was no required education level. Each child pursued education according to the parents' or child's desire. Ednor was four years older than I and only attended until third grade. Some other Labaleine students also quit at Grade 3, thinking they had learned enough to fulfill their aspirations. However, my philosophy is that the sharper the machete, the better it can cut.

On the way home from school, older girls enjoyed tricking me into believing that if I would carry their schoolbooks, I would look smart. Of course, they just wanted relief from carrying their books themselves. Father was concerned that I was up-to-date with my homework, and he kept tabs on me by asking for the date that was on my paper when I came home from school.

On market day I would have enjoyed hanging out with my friends at the market after school, but my father didn't like that. Father would have wanted me to go straight home after school, but usually I spent a little time with a friend on the way. If my father would see me with someone he didn't approve of, he would whip me right on the spot with a branch. On the way home I would sometimes throw stones at turtle doves, guineas, or other small doves. Occasionally I would kill one.

School closed at 3:00 and it was 5:00 by the time I got home. For many years, I got up at 2:30 in the morning to scrape sisal and left for school at 6:30 to arrive by 9:00. In the evenings I would cut sisal leaves to scrape the next morning and retie the animals in the field. I also spent up to two hours every evening doing my homework in the glow of a small kerosene lamp. The fumes from the

School

lamp swirled up and burned in my eyes as I studied. I grew up with only one kerosene lamp in the house.

The main path to the school was the Morne Sainthon, past where cousin Ednor's family now lives, but it was a no-no for me. It was wide and much nicer to walk on than the *dèmòn*, which was very narrow and had branches hanging into the passage. In the morning when the dew was heavy on the leaves, my clothes would get wet, and this was a miserable way to start the school day. Many other students took the Morne Sainthon path, and this was why Father disapproved of it—he didn't want me to walk with the crowd and get into trouble, or be negatively influenced by them.

I was inspired to give education all I had after being exposed to a competitive environment in that first year at Fond-des-Blancs. As a youngster I enjoyed talking about books and about finishing my schooling, while my friends were talking about having the biggest mules, the most goats, and about girls.

Other students who excelled in their studies were an inspiration to me. I enjoyed language, and when I had free time at home, I studied a small book of grammar rules and vocabulary lists. My favorite subject was grammar. I also enjoyed geography.

Plot gardens were a part of the curriculum at the school. The director of the school initiated the plot garden project. Generally, however, the mindset that existed both among the students and teachers was more to attain head knowledge and go to Port-au-Prince and climb the ladder in society than to excel in the less

The Path of Faith

prestigious back-to-the-land life, which is what the plot garden project inherently encouraged. The concept was good, but desire and enthusiasm were wanting.

I attended Fond-des-Blancs in the 1959-60 and the 1960-61 school years. In 1961, Francois Duvalier was reelected president of Haiti. He changed our national constitution so he could proclaim himself president for life. After this, the government schools were closed. My parents never questioned why the Fond-des-Blancs school was closed. When the president spoke, the people listened. I assume the school reopened for the 1961-62 school year, but for fear of the president, parents out in the country were hesitant to send their children to school. In 1963, the school closed again temporarily after the tin roof was taken off by Hurricane Flora. Many of the students from my area didn't attend in the school year after the hurricane. I didn't attend from 1961 to 1965.

In 1966, while Father was working with Mission Union Chretienne and Pastor Ducasse, he sensed the need to send me back to school. Father had probably by then conceived that I would someday be his "reading eyes," since he was unable to read. Community people also encouraged my father to send me to school. In 1966-67, at age 15, I returned to complete Elementary 1. I completed Elementary 2 during the following year. I started Intermediate 1 in the fall of 1968, but my parents pulled me out again after several months because of a drought and shortage of food that made my tuition less affordable.

School

In the 1969-70 school year, with only a full 4th grade and a partial 5th grade education, I taught through Preparatory 2, equivalent to grade 3, in the school held in our church building. MUC sponsored me at $3 (Htn.) per month. I also tutored for several summers.

Even though I had a sporadic school attendance to be able to fill the role of a teacher, I can use the proverb—*A weakened stick is better than two empty hands.*

Antonio Maurisette from La Colline encouraged my father many times to send me to school. Antonio made an offer that if my father could not send me to school, he would. He also offered to take me to his house so I could learn how to sew.

Antonio sold fabric from his house in La Colline. He would board young boys at his house and send them to school. The boys were also able to learn how to tailor if they wanted to. He and his wife had no children, and this was probably part of the motivation for their kindness. Of course, no one would help another unless he was inspired by God. They were very kind and inspirational. Antonio was almost like an angel to me. Antonio chose anyone who was willing to learn. He wanted the boys to be Christians and have a profession. Older boys also helped teach sewing to the younger ones.

My brother Aurel and sisters Clelie, Clement, and Esther began attending school when Emond Prosper from La Colline, sponsored by MUC, was holding classes in our church building. The school was well run with about 50 in attendance. My youngest brother and sister Jovin and Sonya attended all their primary school years in Port-au-Prince.

Later, when I left Labaleine to continue my formal education, I lived almost next door to the school I attended. Then I was able to thank the Lord with a deep-flowing gratefulness for His provision.

Tropical view

8

Miragoane

In January 1971, Pastor Ducasse, the Haitian pastor in charge of the Mennonite mission in Miragoane, asked my parents to send me to the mission headquarters in Miragoane, and he would sponsor my schooling. God was beginning to broaden my horizons, and the path of faith continued.

The first few months I stayed with a family in nearby Desruisseaux and later moved into the upstairs of the church house. It was nice after all those years of sporadic school attendance to live almost next door to a school. I attended the Catholic St. Jean Baptiste School where I was challenged and inspired by my 7th grade teacher, Kelly Damis, who was only three years older than I was.

By this time our church was one of more than 50 churches under Pastor Ducasse's oversight.

While I was in Miragoane, I helped in the youth program at the mission, holding youth meetings on Sunday evening. A few young ladies and I took our turns to lead the worship services. I was involved in this from 1971 to 1974. Services were conducted each Tuesday, Friday, and Sunday evening. Every other Friday evening we would have an all-night prayer service from 10 PM to 5 AM.

Nelson Roes from Castorland, New York, was present at a Sunday morning service and attended the children's Sunday school class that I taught. When each of the classes' offering amounts were read, our class had a few American bills in it. We got extra loud claps for the highest amount. Everyone knew the money came from Nelson, because he was the only American who attended the classes. Nelson was on his first trip to Haiti, on a work team headed by Lester Yancey.

One Sunday evening while the benediction was being given, a truck went by the church, headed toward nearby Desruisseaux. It was the last day of Mardi Gras season, and about 40 or 50 people were on the back of the large straight truck, dancing and playing musical instruments. Some people were even hanging on the side.

At the church we were going around shaking hands and singing the closing song when we heard a thunderous crash and people shouting. Many of the people in the church hurried out to see what had happened. The driver of the truck had been drunk, and failing to turn, he went over the curb above a deep ravine, tipping the truck and dumping all the people. Many were injured and some were killed.

I helped carry injured people to the mission hospital about 500 feet away. It was heart wrenching. Many of us from the church had blood-stained dress clothes by the end of the evening.

During the summer months of 1971, while I was in Miragoane, I was responsible for overseeing some of Pastor Ducasse's rice paddies and sugarcane fields. There were about 35 local people who helped. From a nearby well we channeled water and tried to keep 2 to 3 inches of water in the rice paddies the whole season. When harvest time came, we would use a machete and cut the rice by the handful into 10-gallon baskets.

I finished grade school with grade 7 at St. Jean Baptiste School in June 1972, at the age of 21. At St. Jean Baptiste School I also took middle school, grade 8 and part of 9.

| The Path of Faith

City

9

Port-au-Prince

In 1974, after a few months into grade 9, I moved to Port-au-Prince and finished the school year with a tutor.

Before I left Miragoane, I told Pastor Ducasse of my plans. I told him I wouldn't be able to stay in Miragoane and that I wanted to go to Port-au-Prince to finish my high school.

He said that he was glad that I was doing it, and if I need any help, he will always be there for me. I was very surprised at his response. Because of who he was and the amount of authority he had, this encouragement was special to me, and I still cherish the memory. Pastor Ducasse was a very good translator and inspired me to learn English.

In Port-au-Prince I boarded with Lerines and Ronezi Maignan. I considered them my cousins even though we weren't blood-related. First I attended at Church of God in the city, and later I attended Pastor Christian's church in nearby Carrefour. Pastor Christian was an inspiration to me. He was very sensitive and tenderhearted.

I worked as Sunday school superintendent at the church. I also taught in the church school, teaching Preparatory 1 and 2 and Elementary 1, equivalent to grades 2 to 4 in the U.S. Classes went from 8 to 2:30. In the fall of 1975, I began attending at College Cacique Henry. I attended classes in the evening from 5 to 9 while I taught. During my final two high-school years, I attended College Abraham Lincoln and College Ferdinand Rubbert. (In French, when College precedes the name of a school, it means that it is a private school.)

One day on my way to Abraham Lincoln, I walked past College Quisqueyien and stopped to talk with one of the girls from the church. The school was having a break, and a few ladies had gathered on the school porch. Another girl especially caught my attention. I later asked the girl from the church about her. After this first encounter, I occasionally met up with Rachel Louis Charles, and a small friendship ensued. It seemed to click, but I didn't pursue it for the present. Later, after a two-year lapse in communication, questions clouded our relationship.

All of my high-school education was sponsored by Lester and Darla Yancey from Sarasota, Florida. The Yanceys channeled funds through David Griffinberger of OMS International, Inc., for my high school tuition. David had an office in Port-au-Prince and was the OMS field director. I also did some letter translating for David for supplemental income.

Years later I was asked to preach a short meditation and serve as one of the pallbearers at Lester Yancey's funeral at Bay Shore Mennonite Church in Sarasota.

One Sunday morning I had enough money for the ride on the *taptap,* Haitian public transportation, from the apartment to the church, but I had just one dollar left, enough for the ride home. I felt an urge to drop it into the offering plate, and at the same time I needed it to get back to my apartment. I was fighting within, trying to determine which was most important. I thought of the woman in Scripture who had only one penny and gave it all (Mark 12:42, 43).

When the offering plate came around, I gave the dollar. *Now it is up to me to walk back home,* I thought. After services I started walking. After about half a mile I met a man from Labaleine who was driving a *taptap* from Carrefour to Port-au-Prince; he invited me to ride in the front seat of his vehicle. The Lord had provided—I got a free ride to Port-au-Prince.

In the afternoon I needed to go to a youth meeting at Carrefour, so I borrowed some money from Lerines. When I returned to Port-

And there came a certain poor widow, and she threw in two mites, which make a farthing. ... Verily I say unto you, That this poor widow hath cast more in, than all they which have cast into the treasury: ...

Mark 12:42, 43

au-Prince in the evening, Lerines told me that my father had come for a visit. Nelson Roes from New York also had visited and left a note plus $10 to pay for a *taptap* ride for me to come see him at his motel on the Delmas 19 road.

Nelson wanted me to take a donation to Pastor Christian Eliassaint in Miragoane. The $10 was to pay for the ride to come and see him at the motel and to make the delivery to Miragoane. My father was with me at the motel and said that he was going past Miragoane the next day on his way home and could deliver it for me. With Nelson's approval, Father made the delivery. The rest of the $10 was mine. I believe the reason the tip came was because I gave to the offering plate at the church. The Lord multiplied it.

In 1976, Ronezi, who I boarded with, married my sister Clelie. A few months later I moved in with them in City Soleil.

In July of that year, Andrew Overholt from Indiana came to Haiti to build a schoolhouse for Pastor Debrosse's mission in Paillant, a town located on the mountain above Miragoane. He stayed overnight at my sister Clelie's house where I was boarding. The next day he and I went to the airport to pick up some more of his friends. From the airport we stopped at a grocery store to buy food. While we were in the store a fellow came in asking Andrew and his friends for money. They told him they have no cash, only traveler's checks. The man continued to beg for money. Then he asked me to ask the men for money. I told him not to ask me because he was able to speak English himself, and they had said they didn't have any money.

Finally the cashier asked the man to leave.

The man kept watching us as we walked from the store to our vehicle. Andrew let his friends into the back of the 2-door Honda and I sat in front. When we were ready to leave, the beggar hung on to my door. I rolled down my window to tell him we have to go. He got angry and grabbed me by my shirt collar. I asked him why he's doing this. Without a verbal answer he spat in my face and ran off.

Andrew asked me what I was going to do about it. I said the Bible tells us to turn the other cheek (Matthew 5:39). He may have had a knife and could have been even more dangerous than he already was. We headed for Miragoane.

But I say unto you, That ye resist not evil: but whosoever shall smite thee on thy right cheek, turn to him the other also.

Matthew 5:39

During the school project at Paillant, Abner Overholt, one of Andrew's team members, chose to use an outhouse nearby and ended up dropping his eyeglasses into the hole. Abner had a serious vision impairment and this caused quite a stir for him. With a gallon jug on the end of a long stick we had Abner seeing again!

10

America?

In 1977 I met Melvin Yoder of Hartville, Ohio, who came to Haiti with Willis Miller of Iowa and Clyde Bender of Virginia to drill wells. I knew Willis very well through his involvement in the Miragoane mission and drilling wells. I was living in Port-au-Prince and visited him at his rented house on Delmas 75. Other people were around the house, and Melvin wanted to meet with me privately. We went behind the house to talk.

He asked me what I was doing and of my future plans. In my limited English I told him that I was in my last year in school. I also told him that since my father is a minister of the gospel and basically unable to read, I would like to study the Bible and help my father. I also wanted to improve my English.

He told me that if I were honest and sincere, he would talk to some of his friends to help pay for my Bible school training in the States.

Lester and Darla Yancey were supporting me at the time, with plans to send me to the OMS seminary in Cap Haitien in northern Haiti. However, when the opportunity came to go to America, I took it.

Within a month after Melvin left, I received information and an application from Rosedale Bible Institute of Irwin, Ohio. I took a *taptap* ride to Petionville and had Pastor Eris and Miriam Labady help me fill out the form. Then I returned it to the school. About six weeks later I received my affidavit and I-20 form authorizing me to go to the American Embassy.

I was living with my sister Clelie in City Soleil at the time and got a connecting taxi ride to the embassy building located close to the palace in downtown Port-au-Prince.

Questions were going through my head. *Will my English be good enough? Will I be able to get my visa?*

The high walls surrounding the building were solid concrete, with rolled barbed wire on top. In my hand I had my I-20 international form, noting that Rosedale was qualified to receive foreign students, and my affidavit from Rosedale, ensuring that I had sponsors; plus I had my passport. When my turn came at the gate, the officer looked through the 6" square peephole of the big metal gate and asked me what I needed and asked for my paperwork. After looking through my forms and seeing that everything was in order, he let me in. It was about 7:30 AM. I had arrived at about 4 AM to ensure myself a spot in the line.

The officer also gave me a form to fill out. I felt scared as I walked

America?

into the building. After another person collected my form, I waited in the lobby until an officer from behind the desk called my name. This was my first time in the Embassy building, and I had never seen officers with pistols behind desks.

After my name was called and I answered a few questions, it was only a matter of minutes until the officer had granted me acceptance. I paid my $20 (Htn.) charges to another officer, and he gave me a receipt to bring back in the afternoon to claim my F1 student visa, which allowed me one year of study in the States.

What a wonderful day in my life! The Lord had opened the door for me. People from the church were praying, and the Lord worked it out. I wanted to go to America right away. It was a day of great excitement.

Since I was still attending school in Port-au-Prince, I finished the remainder of the school year and took the required national exam. If I would had stayed in Haiti, I would have taken Philosophie, the grade between high school and college, in the following school year. Since the door of opportunity was open, I took the exam without anxiety. I knew I would go to America whether I passed or not.

Some of my fellow students at the Ferdinand School thought it was foolish that I got a one-year visa to the States but didn't leave right away. I took the national exam in June, and even though I didn't wait on the results, I wanted the satisfaction of having finished the school year.

Before going to the States I returned to Labaleine to spend some time with my family. I also spent a weekend with my friend Albert Antoine, in northern Haiti. He took me to visit the military center at the border between Haiti and the Dominican Republic. We could have sneaked across the border, but I didn't want to get in trouble.

11

Yes, America!

The day of that first and memorable trip from Port-au-Prince, Haiti, to Miami, Florida, USA, was August 25, 1978. It was my first time in a jet and my first time in the United States, both in one day.

Melvin Yoder met me at the airport in Miami. Things looked so different in America. The streets were clean. I was fascinated by all the cars. And where were all the people? In Haiti many people are seen on the roads. Melvin told me that no one walks on the road around here.

After spending the weekend in Sarasota, we started north. Making a few stops along the way, we drove the more than 1,000 miles to Hartville, Ohio. Along the way I noticed a few cars passed us, and Melvin picked up his CB. I thought he was reporting them to the police, but he told me he was just chatting with truck drivers.

One thing that intrigued me after I arrived in Miami was that the American houses weren't built with blocks. Since in Haiti the best-built houses were made with blocks, I imagined that the houses in America would surely be made with blocks as well. I discovered most were framed with wood. I was also intrigued by the insulation used in house construction.

When we arrived in Ohio, I met Melvin's wife, Catherine, and their children, Philip and Freda.

Twelve-year-old Philip helped me learn how to ride a bicycle. He walked beside me and held the bike. After several attempts I wanted to try on my own. I decided if a 12-year-old can master it, then I can too. I was 27. I pushed the bicycle up a hill in front of their house and sat on it and began descending. I did it twice and made it safely. On my third try I took a grand tumble halfway down the hill. I learned later that if you fall while learning to ride a bike, you will be able to do it better after that. That's exactly how it worked for me. My fears had been shaken from me.

I stayed in Melvin Yoder's basement. The first few nights I dreamed over and over that I was going through underpasses. Travel on those big highways had undoubtedly made an impression on me.

A few days after my arrival at the Yoders, I began working with Bill Miller, one of my sponsors, at his vegetable farm in Hartville. I worked there a week or two before I left for Rosedale. I enjoyed working there and learned a lot. I helped load heads of lettuce onto the washer belt to clean them. Melvin and Bill and their wives took me to Rosedale Bible Institute in Irwin, Ohio, about 2½ hours away. Melvin took me to the office and enrolled me. I was amazed by all the books. At this time I just knew enough English to get by.

Before Melvin left, he handed me a checkbook to cover my expenses. I told him I would prefer that someone else write the checks because I didn't know how. He talked to Alvin Miller of the school and asked him to take care of the checkbook for me. Whenever I had a need, I called the Millers. It worked out very well. Alvin and Lovina also took their time to take me shopping for appropriate garments for the winter. Lovina also mended my clothing.

At Rosedale I met Ibrahim Omundi, a student from Kenya, Africa. He was also a first-timer and the first African at the school. I remember Joseph Showalter, now ordained and living in Michigan, staying in the same dorm. He was a barber at Rosedale and enjoyed the feel of my hair.

I spent my first Thanksgiving in the States with the family of a schoolmate, Dale Salenberger, in Chambersburg, Pennsylvania. On our trip back it was getting colder and I asked my friends if we would make it to the school before it snowed. I was afraid that the snow would destroy our vehicle. They laughed when I told them my understanding of snow. I visualized rocks falling and breaking the windshield. The students had a good laugh. We arrived at the school without a problem.

One thing that was new to me when I came to the States was the freedom given to children to do things on their own without consent of their parents.

The Path of Faith

I discovered that as I traveled and spent time with American families, I learned more about the American culture, and this helped me in my studies at Rosedale.

I spent Christmas 1978 with Lester and Darla Yancey of Sarasota, Florida. The Yanceys gave me my first camera on Christmas Day. The Yanceys also hosted other international students at their home for Christmas, through the Christmas House International program. It is a program to provide a family-oriented setting during Christmas break for university students from around the country.

I became special friends with two of the students who stayed at the Yanceys. One of the students who stayed at another home was from Jerusalem. I thought I would ask him questions about the story of Jesus, but since he was a Muslim, he didn't want to talk about it.

Melvin Yoder owned a house in Sarasota and was spending the winter there. He drove one of three vans when the international students went to Disney World.

Three other students and I stayed close together while at Disney. One of the attractions we visited was Space Mountain. After I read the posted sign about Space Mountain, I decided I wouldn't ride it. One of the students thought it would be fun to ride it, but I told him I was afraid. He said that he thought I was a Christian, and that I was supposed to have faith. I gave in.

We each sat in a box seat, fastened our belts, and away we went. Imaginary stars and stones were coming at us. I had my eyes closed most of the time. I was glad when it was over.

I returned to Rosedale to finish the school year. During a cold spell in February, which I wasn't quite adjusted to, I talked with my father on the phone and he said that his prayer would keep me warm. In the summer of 1979 I went to Kalona, Iowa, to visit Willis Miller and Ed Schlabach. I spent the summer staying with Willis Miller's son Leon and his wife Joy and family, and worked with Leon on his water-drilling rig.

Willis and Leon encouraged me to learn how to drive. After I had my permit, Willis let me practice with his Buick. Leon also let me drive his Chevy pickup from his home to the Miller's Well Service office. One morning as I neared the office entrance, a car was coming from the oncoming direction and another from behind. Leon had informed me that Americans are in a hurry, and he didn't want me to get in anyone's way. With a dash I was across the road and missed the driveway completely. When I stopped, the two front wheels were in the ditch. Fortunately, the ditch was shallow enough that I could drive right on through. Leon and I still joke about it. I did manage, though, to get my license that summer.

Actually, I did have a bit of practice earlier, in Haiti, when one of Ronezi's customers from his store in Port-au-Prince let me drive the vehicle he used to do chauffeur work. I actually drove into the booming traffic of Port-au-Prince for a practice round while the other man was in the passenger seat. Embarrassingly enough, I got hung up on the curb, and the other man had to take over. Only later did I realize how risky that trip had actually been.

During my stay at the Millers in the summer of 1979, Leon's three-year-old son, Shaun, asked me to camp out with him. His parents gave us blankets, and we spent a night in their backyard.

After the summer break I returned to Rosedale for my second year.

During Christmas break of 1979, I went to Croghan, New York, with my roommate, Myron Zehr, in his Camaro Z28. I begged Myron to let me drive his car. He allowed me to drive it on a back road near his home. In the following spring I visited his family's sugar bush, where his father collected sap from their more than 4,000 maple trees and processed the syrup. His father asked me to try some syrup by putting it on snow and tasting it. It tasted like fresco.

Later that winter I spent a weekend in Montgomery, Indiana. I stayed with the Abe Knepp family and visited Abe's truss-making business. Paul Knepp, a construction contractor, took me to visit the chicken house he was building. He told me the building would hold 55,000 chickens. I had never seen or heard of anything like it.

My first two years in the United States were very interesting. One Saturday, Nelson Troyer, Elsie Mullet, and Ann Stutzman from the Holmes County, Ohio, area picked me up at Rosedale and took me to visit Ohio Caverns. I had met William Stutzman and his daughter, Ann, in Miragoane and had translated a few times for William when he worked with Pastor Christian's church in

Carrefour. They are like family to me, and usually when I visit Holmes County, I make the Stutzman home one of my stops.

Another memorable event was when Rodney Riegsecker invited me to preach in two churches in Goshen, Indiana. After services, Jonathan Kauffman, also a student at Rosedale, and I drove our separate vehicles back to the school. I was using a vehicle from a fellow student. We had only gone about 35 miles when steam began coming out of the hood of my car. I stopped. Jonathan was behind me and he stopped too. My radiator hose had burst. He was able to trim the hose back with his pocketknife and reattach it. With two gallon jugs we got water at a nearby creek to fill the radiator, and I was on my way again.

In the spring of 1980, in preparation for my return to Haiti, I completed all the courses required to graduate from Rosedale. I sensed the call to be ordained as a preacher of the gospel before I left. All of my sponsors were present at my ordination, which was about a week before graduation.

Ever since I was a very young boy I felt the call to the ministry. I sensed it even more while I worked with my father in the church in Labaleine.

When I was about 16, Elissoi Maignan, a villager, came to our house one day and told my father that the Lord had shown him that He would have His hand on me and that I would someday be a pastor. I was at home at the time and remember this man praying with my father and me before he left. At the time, he was a church leader at the nearby Church of God and is now pastoring in the South American country of Guyana. He was involved in an evangelization effort in our area with lots of praying and speaking in tongues. Our church wasn't involved in it, but many area churches were.

Elissoi and his wife had lived in Labaleine and had five children and adopted an orphan boy. In the late '80s, Elissoi encouraged us at the mission compound to have a high school in Labaleine because he didn't want to send his children to high school in Port-au-Prince.

Today, while he is pastoring in Guyana, he tries to get everyone from Labaleine that comes to his area to come to his church, Christian or not. He's a man full of love. If he asks something of you, it's hard to tell him no.

Elissoi has traveled to the States and lived in both France and Guyana for a long time. Part of the reason Haitians are attracted to France is that they understand French, and also because getting a visa to visit France has generally been easier than getting one to the United States.

I received my diploma from Rosedale Bible Institute in May 1980, after two years studying Bible Theology and Christian Education. At my graduation, ladies from the school cafeteria presented me with a very nice souvenir quilt that I took along back to Haiti.

During my time at Rosedale, I enjoyed going hiking, playing ball, and singing. I also took voice lessons and enjoyed my participation in the school chorus, where I sang bass. We gave numerous programs throughout Ohio. I remember that the song *The Half Has Never Yet Been Told* was especially meaningful to me.

A few times the cooks at Rosedale cooked rice and beans especially for us foreign students.

My two years at Rosedale Bible Institute were difficult and challenging. I took most of my notes in English, but when I got to difficult subjects that I couldn't find English words to express, I switched to French. I sometimes had difficulty following the teacher while he was giving lessons, especially with metaphoric explanations. I relied on the overhead transparencies to make it through the course. Book reports helped me improve my grades the first year. My main mission in the States was to study theology and improve my English. I felt my time at Rosedale was well spent.

The persons who sponsored my two years at Rosedale were Melvin Yoder, Willis Miller, Eli Helmuth, William Miller, Henry Bontrager, Edwin Schlabach, and Crist Helmuth. I am most grateful for their generosity.

The week following my graduation, Lonnie Martin, a friend I met at Rosedale, offered to take me to Canada with him. We attended the wedding of one of Lonnie's friends in Kingston, Ontario. Our next stop was at Montreal. We spent the weekend there and did some sightseeing. On Sunday we visited a Haitian church that had a Canadian pastor. Lonnie and I both spoke in the church. I translated to French for Lonnie. We didn't know where we would

The Path of Faith

spend the night, but the pastor at the church told us of a pastor in Quebec City that would provide lodging for us. When we arrived in Quebec City, we phoned to the pastor's house, but he wasn't at home. The person who answered told us they would not lodge strangers.

After driving around the city, we happened upon a church having Bible study. We joined the Bible study and upon invitation from one of the church members, we spent the night in a schoolhouse nearby.

We visited the Parliament in Ottawa and the town of Joliette. In Saint Catherine, Ontario, we visited a friend who worked with Grace Children's Hospital in Haiti. We also visited Niagara Falls.

In Kitchener we visited Shirley Martin, a former Rosedale schoolmate, before heading back to Ohio.

Lonnie dropped me off at William Stutzmans in Sugarcreek, where I had left my luggage. He headed back to his home in Kansas. Today he is married to a German lady and still lives in Kansas.

12

Haiti Again

In accordance with my promise to Melvin and my other sponsors, I returned to Haiti after two years at Rosedale.

William Stutzman and his daughter, Ann, and I boarded the plane in Cleveland, Ohio, and flew to Miami, Florida, where we met Myron Dietz and John Strickler coming from Lancaster, Pennsylvania. We traveled together to the Port-au-Prince airport, where my father, Pastor Christian Maisonneuve, and Pastor Eris Labady welcomed us.

Myron Dietz was scheduled to speak on Anabaptist history at the church in Carrefour. I had first met him when he conducted seminars at Rosedale while he was on sabbatical from Lancaster Mennonite High School, where he taught for a number of years.

In Haiti I looked for ways to implement what I had learned. I held seminars at several schools and churches, using material and gleanings from the IBLP Basic Youth Conflicts Seminar that I had attended in Dayton, Ohio, while attending at Rosedale.

The Path of Faith

For a few months I rented one of Eris Labady's rooms in Petionville. Eris and I had our membership at the church in Carrefour and shared the vision of helping and improving the living conditions of our own people.

I conducted seminars on Christian living at area churches, with the first one at Gospel Light Chapel in Carrefour, where I also helped with preaching. I was also responsible for chapel at Son Light Mission School in Croix-des-Bouquets (Santo) southeast of Titanyen, where I spoke about Bible characters.

While teaching at the Son Light school I enjoyed asking people questions on my *taptap* trips. With the guidance-counseling course that I took at Rosedale and the Youth Conflicts Seminar I attended, I wanted to learn more about people.

One morning after my one-hour chapel at the Santo school, I gave an invitation. Of the more than 100 students and teachers, four or five boys stood and wanted to give their hearts to the Lord. It was especially meaningful to me when one of the boys spoke out boldly and said that both his parents were witch doctors. The teachers and I laid hands on the boys and prayed for them.

I was in Haiti for ten months. I used my teaching skills and also helped out at the children's home at Leogane, driving their VW mini-van and hauling in supplies from town. At the home, I worked with Ben and Drucilla Yoder of Stuarts Draft, Virginia. After I began working at Leogane, I used the van to go to Son Light.

Haiti Again

The Path of Faith

Joel

Rachel

13

Rachel

During the two years that I had spent in America, I had lost contact with Rachel Louis Charles. One day after I started driving the van at Leogane and was on my way to Son Light, I saw her standing at the end of her street waiting for a *taptap*. I pulled over and talked to her and ended up taking her to the radio station in Port-au-Prince where she worked as secretary.

At first she reluctantly accepted a ride when I offered. She didn't know whether I was the same man she had known before. She didn't know whether I was married or possibly engaged. We soon discovered we were in the same boat.

I asked Rachel about the letters I had sent and why I hadn't gotten a reply. She seemed surprised by the question and then explained that during my two years in the States, she hadn't heard from me—not even once. She couldn't understand it. Actually, I had written a number of letters and sent them to her friend because she didn't have an address. Her friend never gave her my letters. During my time in the States, Rachel had asked her friend whether she had heard from me. She said she didn't, and ran off.

For about four or five months I picked up Rachel and took her to work on my way to Santo. I was ready to begin a relationship, but I had unanswered questions. *She's attending a Seventh Day Adventist Church. Her parents don't agree with our relationship, and she's working at a secular radio station.* I prayed that if my feelings were for real and if this was something the Lord wanted for me, then I wanted Him to make it clear. I asked God for a sign.

She mentioned to me on Friday that she was going to the beach with her radio station co-workers on Sunday. When I heard this, I thought it would be inappropriate to be dating a girl who would go on a picnic with non-Christians on a Sunday morning. I didn't think it would be fair to me. *If you want me to date this girl, you must give me a clear understanding,* I prayed.

On Saturday I went to Pastor Christian's church to hold an adult Bible study. I returned home around 9:00 in the evening. My relationship with Rachel was weighing heavily on my mind, and I finally gave it to the Lord.

I went to bed about 10:30. Around midnight there was a knock at the gate of the Leogane compound. I went out through pouring rain and nearly knee-deep water to meet a group of about 13 people from Minnesota. They asked me to take them to the nearest telephone booth to make a call.

They tried calling to the Christianville mission compound but were unable to connect, so we went back to the children's home, and they spent the night there. In the morning I guided them to Christianville.

It is actually common in Haiti that when it rains everyone stays at home, especially in the rural areas, no matter if it's Sunday or the middle of the week. I didn't realize that God would use the rain to answer my prayer. This was the day that Rachel was planning to picnic at the beach with her friends.

It rained all night and all day Sunday. Nobody went to church.

On the following Monday and Wednesday, I gave Rachel a ride, but we didn't discuss the picnic. The second week one of the fellows that was riding with us asked her about the picnic. She said she didn't go. I asked her why not. She said it was because of the rain.

I was very happy to hear that. Now I was ready to talk to her parents about dating.

When I discussed dating with her, she feared that since she was Seventh Day Adventist, it would cause a problem with my parents.

I met with her parents and expressed my interest in their daughter. I said I would take full responsibility for her. This would affirm to them that I respected her and would be kind to her. It would also make the parents responsible to not let another fellow date her. I also made sure I told them that I was going to school, which is an important qualification to gain the respect of a girl's parents.

Typically, the shortest dating period for Haitians is about 5 years and the longest is 15. One girl in our church married after dating for 14 years. Seldom is the dating period shorter than 5 years.

Her parents gave their blessing. This was December 1980.

In March of 1981, after I got a new visa to go to the States, her parents said they couldn't keep Rachel for me. They said that I have to get married before I go. I said I couldn't do that. I didn't want to get married in the Seventh Day Adventist church, and I didn't think my parents would have liked it either.

14

America Again

During the ten months I spent in Haiti, I decided that sharing the gospel is sometimes not enough. I discovered that Christians in Haiti who own land are willing to work. I decided that persons who evangelize must also know how to help improve living conditions and develop agricultural skills. I especially aspired to work with church leaders.

In April of 1981, I returned to the States with plans to attend an agricultural school. I didn't have an agricultural school lined up, so the Yanceys paid for a spring term at Rosedale Bible Institute for me in the meantime. During my six-week term at Rosedale, I longed for Rachel to come to the States as well. Though Rachel and I had not discussed it previously, I called Willis Miller of Kalona, Iowa, and told him of my desire for Rachel to come to Rosedale. Willis was immediately supportive, and I got application forms from the Institute and sent them to Pastor Eris in Haiti for her. I made a note for Pastor Eris to contact Rachel at the radio station and tell her about it.

The Path of Faith

John Strickler, who I met on my first return trip to Haiti, made arrangements for me to visit him in Lancaster, Pennsylvania, in May after spring term. After a short visit, I flew to Sarasota.

I spent the summer of 1981 working on Lester and Darla Yancey's 1400-cow dairy farm in Myakka City, Florida. It was a good experience. The Yanceys were like parents to me. I learned many things from the Yanceys, and one thing I remember from Darla was to give good gifts to other people and not just leftovers. This is how she treated me and taught me by example. That summer on the farm was a great blessing to me.

I saved the $1200 that I earned on the farm that summer, determined to attend agricultural school. By the end of the summer the Yanceys' county extension agent had helped me find Abraham Baldwin Agricultural College (ABAC) in Tifton, Georgia. I sent my application to ABAC and was accepted. From Sarasota I took a Greyhound bus to Tifton.

After I arrived, I called a taxi and asked him to take me to the cheapest motel close to ABAC. He said that motels are expensive around there, but he knew of a rescue mission. I didn't know what a rescue mission was, but when I heard "mission," I expected it to have something to do with missionaries and thought it would be okay.

I went to the front desk to register. This is when I discovered what a rescue mission was. I was scared. I asked the person at the desk if I could go out for a moment. Even though I didn't know where else I would go, I wanted to leave and not return.

The registrar said if I left I couldn't return. I decided to stay. I went to my room and put my briefcase under my head to guard it. There were two bunk beds in the room, and my roommates smelled of alcohol. A few were drunk. I slept with "one eye open and one eye closed"—I didn't want my summer savings stolen. I could hardly wait to see daylight.

In the morning I got a taxi ride to the school, only to discover I was about a week early. After talking with some people on the campus, I secured an empty bed in the dorm with a plastic mattress. The empty school building reminded me of a ghost town. There were no pillows and no sheets on the bed. Even though it was cold and I could hardly sleep, I felt safer than I did at the rescue mission. The next day I walked to Tifton with my bag on my shoulder and bought sheets and a pillow.

The following week I registered at the school. I took the $1200 cash to the registrar's office. They told me they could not accept cash, only checks. They suggested I deposit the money at the bank and open a checking account so I could write a check. I had never written a check in my life.

When I arrived at the bank, they asked me for identification. I had my passport, my driver's license from Iowa, and my international license, but I was missing a Social Security number. The next stop was the Social Security office. Finally, I was able to open a checking account.

I paid for my first quarter tuition and books, my private room, and a small refrigerator. The private room cost more, but the public dorm would close during holidays, and I would have no other place to stay. I had $150 left, so I bought bread, bologna, peanut butter, mayonnaise, and Kool-Aid—my menu for three months. This was all I could afford.

At ABAC I majored in agriculture. I began to understand corn pollination during the soil/plant course. I remembered seeing the farmers in Haiti cut the tassels from corn after pollination; to produce larger ears, they had said. I learned about pollination and the production of hybrids. I also learned about flood, sprinkle, and drip irrigation methods.

I remember Dr. Sebet at ABAC smoked lots and lots of cigarettes. When he said something that he wanted us to remember, he said, "This is gospel."

15

Rachel to America

It was an exciting day at the radio station when Pastor Eris Labady stopped in and broke the news of the opportunity for Rachel to come to the States so we could be together.

A few months later, after all her forms had been returned and she had gotten her passport, she made the historical trip to the American Embassy to get her visa. When she got to the Embassy, she noticed that everyone else had fat envelopes of documents and necessaries to get their visas. She felt a little intimidated with her small packet. The agent took her documents, and after looking at them, said he's sorry, but he can't give her a visa. He stamped "denied" on her passport. She didn't give up too easily. She asked him why she is being denied and what she was missing. She explained that her sponsor had already paid all her tuition. She said that her sponsor either needs to get a reimbursement from the school or she needs to tell her sponsor what she needs so he can send it.

Many people were praying during this time that she would get her visa. The agent wasn't able to give her a satisfactory explanation. After reexamining her forms, the agent actually accepted her appeal and she got her visa. How exciting for her! The Lord is faithful indeed.

During my time with Lester and Darla in the summer of 1981, I met Keith and Clara Starkey, who were good friends of the Yanceys. After I discovered they were the owners of Agape Flights, I asked Keith if he could bring Rachel to the States. Agape Flights was, and still is today, the mail carrier for missionaries in Haiti, transporting parcels from the Starkey office in Sarasota to the Port-au-Prince airport. Keith graciously transported Rachel on her first unforgettable flight in August of 1981 in their four-passenger plane for a meager $50.

Could we have worked all this out on our own? No, God was with us.

Rachel spent her first two months with Frank and Marian Overholt in Sarasota. She began the fall term at Rosedale Bible Institute of Irwin, Ohio in October.

16

Tifton

Rachel and I were dating. We were both in the States now, but she was all the way up in Ohio and I was in Georgia. I began brainstorming ideas of how we could be closer together.

Rachel had an interest in nursing, and I knew that Rosedale did not offer courses with eligible credits to use toward nursing. I concluded that she should move to Georgia and we should get married, then she could take courses toward nursing at ABAC. I felt it would be inappropriate for us to attend the same school and live in the same area unless we got married.

Before I called Rachel with my ideas, I decided I should first find a pastor to marry us. I took a walk one day trying to find the Church of God in Tifton, since I had attended the Church of God in Port-au-Prince. In the phone book I found that the church was on Tift Ave. I found Tift, but I went south and should have gone north. The church was closer than I thought. The best way I can explain what happened next is with Romans 8:28. ...*All things work together for good to them that love God, to them who are the called according to His purpose.*

"Where are you from, young man?" called a man working in his garden beside the road. I began walking toward him. He asked more questions. I told him my name and that I'm from Haiti. He asked me what I was doing there. After I told him I was enrolled at ABAC, he introduced himself as Jack Ratcliffe and said he's an agriculture specialist for the state of Georgia. I was astounded.

He asked whether I had pictures from Haiti with me, and invited me to visit his church. Jack attended the Trinity United Methodist church. Unknown to me, this would be the first step of an important and lasting relationship with the Methodists at Trinity.

I continued my search for the Church of God. I asked the pastor to marry us, but he didn't think it was proper because we were students and not legal citizens. Later, one Sunday evening, I walked to Jack's home and attended the Methodist church with him. I decided to see what Jack's pastor had to say.

Jack Ratcliffe told the congregation a little about me and how we met. Some people in the church were surprised when they saw me, because I was the first black person to enter their church building. Pastor Charles Ricks asked if I have something to share. I shared my testimony. Coincidently, he had been in Petit Goave, Haiti, two years before on a work project.

After the evening service, Pastor Charles Ricks and his wife, Nuana, along with Pastor Vernon Edwards and his wife, Evelyn,

Tifton

Jack and Frances Ratcliffe, Jack and Bobbie Bailey, Hallman and Ivy Hasty, Eddy Willie, and Nell Carter invited me to accompany them to a fancy restaurant for a social gathering. I told them I didn't have a way to get back to the college, but they offered me a ride. They ordered only enough food to socialize over. They asked me if I was interested in having coffee. I told them I don't drink coffee.

Pastor Rick's wife asked if I would like a piece of pie. After I hesitated, she asked if I wanted a hamburger. A hamburger? I dared not show my intense eagerness. I had not eaten cooked food for three months. All I had been able to afford was bread, bologna, peanut butter, mayonnaise, and Kool-Aid. She asked me what I ate at the dorm, but I hesitated to answer. She said I should go ahead and eat. I chomped away on my hot, tasty hamburger, the first in months. The Lord was pouring out His blessing on me. It felt like heaven had come down.

They asked me why I lived alone. I told them that I would like for us to get married, but the pastor I talked to said he wouldn't marry us. I explained that I felt living together in an unmarried state is living in sin. Pastor Vernon assured me that getting married was the right thing to do, and that he couldn't understand why it couldn't be done. He sounded pretty confident.

I called Rachel while she was on term break from Rosedale, visiting a friend in New York. I gave her my ideas about her schooling and the arrangements for getting married that I had been working on. She was happy about it and wedding bells began to ring.

We sent wedding invitations to our parents and friends. In the meantime I talked with Pastor Eris, who lived in Petionville, Haiti, sharing the news with him, and asked him to have my father call me. Father was very happy when I told him the news. I told him to tell Rachel's parents also.

Two weeks before the wedding, Rachel had her first Greyhound bus ride, from Rosedale to Tifton. Lots of things were already planned before she arrived.

After the social gathering at the restaurant, Jack and Bobbie took me back to the college in their Lincoln. They asked me more details about the school, and I told them what I was eating.

The next morning while I was in English class my foreign advisor, who was also my English teacher, handed me a note. The note was from Dr. Bridges, the dean of the college, requesting that I come to his office. In Haiti we use the French word for dean, *doyen*, to mean a lawyer. I had never been called to the dean's office before. I was afraid I had done something wrong and would be sent back to Haiti.

When I arrived at the dean's office, I saw Pastor Ricks and Pastor Vernon. *At least I have their support,* I thought.

They told me they had been talking to Dr. Bridges and had talked to Jack and Bobbie after the evening before and found out what I had to eat. They asked me how many meals I would like at the cafeteria each day.

I told them that I didn't have any money to pay for meals. Pastor

Ricks told me the church committee had decided to pay for my meals. "Praise the Lord!" I said. This was a big shock. I told them that two meals would be fine, one at noon and one at night. *In the morning I can chew on my bread*, I thought. I felt very unworthy of the Lord's blessing. Before they left, they bought me enough meal tickets for the entire school year.

On break I told my friend Wilfred Shannon from Monrovia, Liberia, about it. He could hardly believe that there was a church in Tifton, Georgia, that would be so kind.

He told me he went to a church in Tifton and that the people were very discriminating. I told him that I'm sure he will find that in some churches but that I have found a church that I don't think is so.

Since I knew Wilfred was having difficulty finding food, I told him I would share the meal tickets with him. One of us would eat at noon and the other in the evening. Whenever he was not in his room, I would slip the meal ticket under the door to make sure he got his meal for the day.

One Sunday morning Wilfred asked me if he could visit the church that had given the meal tickets. Jack and Bobbie picked us up at the college. Because of Wilfred's previous experiences, he was very critical of any church. One visit to Trinity, though, made him want to attend regularly.

A few weeks later Wilfred gave his testimony. Before he was finished, most of the people were in tears. Wilfred told them that during his Christian life, this was the first time that he had found a caring church.

He asked to be baptized and become a member. Wilfred and a few others from the church were later immersed at a church member's swimming pool. It was such a blessing.

In a Monday evening Bible study we had a unique feet-washing experience. Someone in the church that opposed feet washing in communion offered to wash our feet. The person, though doubtful of the need for feet washing in communion, offered that Wilfred, Rachel, and I are doing mission work that they can't do and our feet are going to go places they can't go. The person felt an urge from God to wash our feet. We had feet washing for everyone. This was very touching and we felt unworthy.

I shared with the other foreign students that I had found a caring church. Eventually, there were about 20 students who wanted to attend with us. I was using a Pontiac that Marvin Beiler from Meigs, Georgia, had given to me to use. When the Pontiac was getting full, Pastor Ricks offered me the church van to transport the students from the college. It became a ministry to the foreign students.

The church always had a social time on Wednesday evening after prayer meeting, with tea and coffee. Later the ladies in the church began providing a special meal on Wednesday evenings for the international students. On holidays some of the families of the church prepared special meals for the students and entertained them in their homes. On Sunday noon families took foreign students to their homes for lunch.

Vernon and Evelyn Edwards helped us find a place to live. Since Evelyn was a schoolteacher, she knew a lot of people in Tifton. She had heard of a house complex being built south of town. She decided to take us there. When we arrived, they told us the houses were being built for U.S. citizens. Though we were students, we still applied. A short time later Evelyn received notice that we qualified, not only to have a home, but also for the program to have our utility bills paid because of our low income. The only income we had was a promissory note from one of our sponsors. The Tifton church put in a table and chairs for us. Again, the Lord provided.

With all the blessings, Pastor Ricks said, "Joel, you must have a big faith to make these things happen." I told him of Melvin Yoder's encouragement to write a book. When the pastor asked me how I would title the book, I told him, *The Path of Faith*. The pastor's observation confirmed my idea for a book title.

I called Lonnie Martin to share the news of the upcoming wedding. About 1½ years prior to that we had traveled to Canada together. He told me he was leaving soon to go to Germany to do mission work. Soon after our phone call I was surprised to receive a money order in the mail from Lonnie. At the time when I had called Rachel about getting married, I had had only $12 in my possession. The Lord was carrying us.

Jack and Bobbie Bailey asked me whether I had bought my wedding suit. At first I didn't want to tell them. It turned out though that they had a surprise up their sleeve. The TV manufacturing company Jack worked for had sent him a complete suit as a gift, but it was too small for him. One Monday evening before Bible study, I went to the Baileys and tried it on. It fit perfectly. Bobbie was so excited that God had worked this out, and she shared it at the Bible study with an emphatic "Hallelujah."

The secretary who worked for Hallman Hasty at his airplane communication systems shop was getting married and had already bought her wedding dress. She kindly offered that Rachel could borrow hers instead of renting one. Rachel tried it on and it fit perfectly.

The bridesmaids were planning to rent dresses. When they arrived at the rental store, there were only three dresses left, and each one fit each of the girls just right. This was exciting for the church prayer group members.

Could all this have been just merely coincidental?

We were married at Trinity United Methodist Church on December 26, 1981. Best man was Hallman Hasty, a good friend from the church. Pastor Eris' brother Dorlus was groomsman. He was working in Sarasota at the time and was the only Haitian guest at the wedding. Ware Gardener was also groomsman. Maid of honor was Lisa Bailey, who is now married to Clyde Thompson. Bridesmaids were Lori Cooper and Malinda Ricks.

Pastor Vernon Edwards and Pastor Charles Ricks preached our

wedding sermon with Pastor Ricks performing the ceremony. Over the years the Methodist church has moved Pastor Ricks a number of times, but we have tried to stay in contact.

Ware Gardener's wife, Carol, was a good friend of Rachel's and gave her $20 on our wedding day. Instead of going on a honeymoon after the wedding, we took the money and went to a Holiday Inn restaurant in Tifton.

At the wedding reception we had finger foods and cake that was prepared by the church ladies. Since we married on the day after Christmas, there were lots of poinsettias in the church, and it didn't require a lot of decorating.

The group who paid for my schooling at Rosedale gave me a check of $390, the leftover money from the schooling fund, on our wedding day.

Tifton is a golden memory.

We always called Frank Overholt's wife, Marian, "Mom." Before Frank and Marian left the wedding, Marian told me to find Rachel and tell her she wants to say good-bye. I looked everywhere and couldn't find her. All the while Rachel was lying behind Marian's seat in their car where she had told Rachel to hide. We had a lot of fun with Marian.

Marian gave me my first English/French dictionary while in Miragoane. After that, I began learning one new English word each day. I worked very hard to learn English correctly. In my spare time I practiced with the American volunteers at the mission. If I came across a new word, I grabbed my dictionary.

Frank and Marian Overholt are the parents of Pastor Eris Labady's wife, Miriam, and both have now passed away. I had met the Overholts through Miriam in Miragoane, where Marian taught a baking and cooking class for young girls.

Rachel and I were both attending school together and had some difficulties paying for our schooling. Since I had shared with John Strickler my vision to learn some agricultural techniques to help farmers in Haiti, I wrote to him and explained the need to pursue my studies in this field. His reply was that we should let them know what we needed, because we can help the Haitian people better than they can. From that time the River Brethren paid for my training in agriculture through ABAC, as well as Rachel's prerequisites for nursing at ABAC. They continued their support for me while I attended Hesston College and for Rachel until she finished her nursing degree at Florida International University in Miami.

17

Kansas

ABAC is a state college and could not accept our Bible credits from Rosedale. I spoke to Myron Deitz about the situation. He said Hesston College in Kansas has a good agricultural program and will accept my credits from Rosedale.

In the summer of 1982, Willis Miller, Rachel, and I spent 6 weeks traveling through the U.S. to launch Water for Life, which is today a large well-drilling organization in Haiti. We spoke and showed slides in churches, starting in Florida and traveling as far north as Boston and as far west as Nebraska. The trip gave Rachel and me a chance to see our old friends and meet new people.

After our tour, Rachel and I drove from Willis' home in Kalona, Iowa, to Tifton, Georgia, to pick up our belongings to move to Kansas. We used Willis' car, a VW Rabbit, and packed it so full I couldn't use the rearview mirror.

We stayed in Alvin and Gertrude Blough's basement for the first school year. Alvin owned a styrofoam manufacturing company and taught chemistry at Hesston. We had a great time at the Bloughs. They were like parents to us. I enjoyed helping Alvin cut wood in the winter. After the school year we moved into a house trailer in Hutchinson.

During our stay we became friends with Cliff and Liz Bitikoffer, whose daughters, Kathleen and Dena, were missionaries in Haiti. The Bitikoffers were very kind to us. They allowed us to use their Honda car for transportation when we needed it.

We also met Edgar and Marge Harms, who had spent some time in Haiti with MCC. They were very supportive and gave us a lot of encouragement.

We met Orlan and Anna Belle Becker from the Canton area. We hadn't met them personally in Haiti, but because they and their teenage son had been missionaries in Haiti, we got together occasionally.

In 1968, I met Ivan Miller, a Mennonite minister from Hutchinson, Kansas, at a church conference while I lived in Miragoane. We visited him and began attending the Plainview Church where he pastored. We also attended Maranatha Church pastored by Paul Nisley, on some weekends. I was asked to preach a number of times at these churches. For several months, until we had our own vehicle, a couple from one of the two churches would give us a ride to church services each Sunday morning. We lived about 40 miles from each of the churches.

One evening, John and Sylvia Nisley came to visit us. They

brought bags and bags of groceries that were collected for us from the two churches. It was enough food to last for three months.

In January 1983, Jonas Nisley told me that his sister and brother-in-law, Ervin and Emma Stutzman, had visited Haiti and that he wanted us to meet them. So one Sunday after services, my wife and I had the privilege of visiting Ervin and Emma, who were the owners of Stutzman's Greenhouse in Hutchinson. We didn't realize that the Stutzmans would later play a very key role in the growth and development of the mission in Labaleine.

One branch of the agricultural course at Hesston was animal reproduction. This took me to the Colorado State Fair in Denver in 1983. That really opened my eyes. I had never seen anyone clipping and shampooing animals before.

At Hesston I learned the difference between high technology and appropriate technology. On one project I drew a diagram configuring an irrigation system to capture water during the night from the spring south of the mission in Labaleine. I had measured the water once at 50 gallons per minute. I would want the running water to flow into a cistern at night. Then, as a school project, in the fields below we would lease a field from a landowner and have school children care for small plots and irrigate them with the captured water.

Another thing that I would like to see implemented in Haiti is an irrigation system with a barrel set under the rain gutter of the house and a hose down to water a plot garden. Possibly we can initiate and encourage more gardening closer to home, since all food is currently raised in a field away from home.

The first year in Kansas, Rachel attended at Hesston and the following year she moved to JUCO, a junior college in Hutchinson.

Rachel's interest in nursing started when she was about nine years old. A nicely dressed nurse, with her white hat and starched white garb, who lived down the street from Rachel's family, would walk past her family's house every day. She longed for the same fulfilling life that she imagined in that nurse. Rachel's philosophy is that you need to have God first and then a determined 'I can do it' attitude.

Rachel knew some Spanish that she had learned in school in Port-au-Prince, but very little English. She learned English in school in the States and from practicing it with the church ladies. More than once, Rachel was frustrated with English and her courses. I encouraged her to 'hang in there.'

Jack and Bobbie Bailey paid our airfare to Atlanta to spend Christmas 1982 with them in Tifton. Pastor Edwards and Jack Bailey drove 2½ hours from Tifton to the airport to pick us up.

Bobbie had just bought a brand new Buick with about 15 miles on it. She knew we had friends in the area and offered us her car. She also gave us her credit card to buy gas.

After our time together, Hallman Hasty, who owns a private airplane, flew us from Tifton to the Atlanta airport. We also spent Christmas 1983 with the Baileys. The Tifton people hold a warm place in our hearts.

On the Friday after Thanksgiving 1983, Rachel and I took our little

Ford Pinto, with a shovel and some blocks in the back for traction, and headed for Dallas Center, Iowa. We were planning to spend the weekend with Old Order River Brethren friends.

When we came near to Leon, Iowa, it was snowing. We stopped to call Bishop Philip Funk of Dallas Center to find out the condition of the road, because we had heard that an ice storm was coming. Though it was snowy and wintry, he told us the road was passable. He did not realize though, that I was not a good driver on snow and ice. From Kansas to Leon, Iowa, the road was good. However, as we approached Des Moines only one lane was open, but it was coated with glaring ice. We both had our seat belts on and were slowly inching along to avoid an accident. In my rearview mirror I saw that a semi-truck and a pickup were gaining on us and there was no room for them to pass. When they got close to us, I attempted to get to the side of the road, but found that I couldn't let them pass. Suddenly I lost control of the vehicle and our car headed for the ditch. I told Rachel, "This is the end." I braked and the car spun around twice. In the meantime, the semi-truck and pickup had managed to get around us, and I regained control of the car and was able to move on. We spent the night in a motel, concerned that it may not be wise to continue.

We spent some time with Philip's family and his parents, Stanley and Norma Funk. We had planned to worship with them on Sunday, but after hearing on the radio that another ice storm was on its way, we decided to drive home instead. The storm had begun by the time we arrived at our trailer in Hutchinson.

The Path of Faith

Recess

18

School in Labaleine!

From September 23-25, 1983, the Mennonite Disaster Service reunion was held in Mount Ridge, Kansas, celebrating a 20-year presence in Haiti.

Enos Miller, who was part of the team that went to Haiti in 1963, invited us. Enos and Mary Miller, Ervin and Emma Stutzman, and Rachel and I attended. Each MDS volunteer shared his or her experiences while building houses in Côtes-de-Fer. They also asked me to share my experiences during Hurricane Flora. We had a wonderful weekend together.

They took an offering and gave the $585 to us to use at our discretion. We asked the group whether it would be okay to use it toward building a school in Labaleine. We felt fortunate to have gotten all the help we received to enable us to go through school, and felt responsible to help others. They gave their blessing on the idea, and I requested that Ervin Stutzman be responsible to put the money in the bank until it reached the needed amount to build the schoolhouse. To see a school in Labaleine had been a dream of mine for a long time. This was the beginning of MDS Haiti.

When I was about 18, I had decided that someone should do something about the lack of education and the rejection that the Labaleine people experienced. People from other communities considered Labaleine people to be very primitive—and perhaps a little simpleminded. When Labaleine people were asked to sign something, they would just write an "X" on the document. It was like a curse on the people. The Labaleine people were rejected. There was a sort of chant going—*Their skin color is normal, but being able to write something and think right—far be it*. When lawyers and land surveyors would come to the Labaleine community, which includes the nearby villages of Kay Chalin and Trompe, they knew they could make money on them, because people weren't able to read and write.

The reunion was held in September. In November, I called Pastor Eris in Haiti and told him to tell my Father to call me. When Father called I told him the news that we're going to build a school in Labaleine. Father was excited to hear that. He said he had sensed for a long time that it was coming. This was the last time I would talk with my father.

Father returned to Labaleine with the school idea and talked to Lexines Maignan, who started holding classes in the church building.

Ervin talked to people about the school project, and the fund began to grow. We had pencils made with Psalm 119:57 imprinted on

School in Labaleine!

them in French that were passed to the children in the community.

As a part of my agricultural studies at Hesston, I did my internship with Ervin at Stutzman's Greenhouse. A banana plant someone had given to Ervin became a good promotion medium for the school. I used half of a whiskey barrel, cut holes in for ventilation, and transplanted the banana plant. I put it in one of the greenhouses and fertilized it. It took off. I cut off the first little sucker that came up the side and transplanted it. After it was growing very nicely, a lady who came to the greenhouse bought it for $15. In Haiti it would probably have cost about 2¢ (Htn.). I transplanted two more shoots, and they were sold for $30 each. Along with this the mother plant produced a hanger with over 200 bananas. On the day of open house at the greenhouse Henry Nisly offered that he would buy one banana for a dollar. That gave Ervin an idea and he posted a sign to sell the fruit and the funds would go to Haiti. Many bananas were sold. A local radio station covered the greenhouse event and the Hutchinson News and TV ended up running stories on the project. A kind lady from western Kansas read the newspaper story and sent a contribution.

Thou art my portion, O Lord: I have said that I would keep thy words.

Psalm 119:57

The Path of Faith

After a tragic accident had claimed my father's life, I traveled to Haiti with Ervin Stutzman and others, and we looked for a building site for the school.

Ervin took an increasing interest in the work, and we made several trips to Haiti together. After seeing the needs and with a strong desire to serve the needs of the Labaleine people, Ervin and Emma Stutzman moved to Labaleine, Haiti, in September 1989.

The Stutzmans were in the process of selling their greenhouse business, and, as a part of their retirement plans, they were considering mission work with Mennonite Central Committee (MCC) when the opportunity came up to work in Labaleine, Haiti.

At first they moved into the small cement-block house with my mother. Quite different from the States, cooking was done outdoors, the shower stall was a small enclosure outdoors, and living quarters were a bit cramped.

In the meantime, Ervin coordinated the building of the VS unit. While this project had still been in the planning stages, some Americans encouraged Ervin to add a second level for living quarters for themselves. This worked out very well. They boarded with Mother for the first fifteen months before moving. The lower level was then used for Emma's sewing classes that were started at Mother's house and for Ervin's workshop. With Ervin's interest and experience in greenhouses, he also built a small greenhouse on the compound with plans to encourage food-plant production and tree planting for the community.

School in Labaleine!

During the time of the early construction projects, our family was living in Miami, Florida. With our plans to move to Labaleine, Ervin began coordinating the building of the clinic in 1993, with a clinic at ground level and living quarters on the second story.

In 1994, the two-story, 40' x 80' foot Dorcas Center building was begun to give the well-received but crowded sewing classes more space. Plus it would accommodate the workshop, a storage depot, guest quarters, and rooms for the secondary school classes. Since then, other building projects have included a school office addition to the clinic and two cisterns.

Through Ervin and Emma's faithfulness, and with the assistance of others, many of the local ladies now own their own sewing machine and are able to sew for their families and others in the community.

Ervin and Emma, through Haitian Relief and Missions, have been very instrumental in the development of Labaleine. The Stutzmans were in their 60s at the time of their move, and in April 1998, 14 years since the beginning of their involvement, stepped down from the day-to-day administrative responsibilities. On behalf of the Labaleine community, I want to express my gratitude to the Stutzmans for this monumental contribution to all the people of Labaleine.

Funds that were accumulated in the States for the school building were sent to my brother-in-law, Ronezi Maignan and his brother, Victorin who coordinated the project along with a few other local men.

The official Labaleine school opened in October 1984, with a 300-student capacity and 144 students attending the first year. By 1999, enrollment had exceeded 450 and a partial second story was added.

While the school was being built in Labaleine, the locals thought we were foolish. *There's a school in Fond-des-Blancs, why put a school in Labaleine? It won't work*, they said.

Today they want their children to be in the school. *Please take our four-year-old for us*, they say.

This is not a financially profitable venture. My interest is in seeing the community get on its feet and seeing people respect and worship God and be prosperous in the Lord.

Jean Thomas's wife, Joy, runs the school near Fond-des-Blancs. We are very close friends to them. In 1998, she said she didn't think there was a need for students from Labaleine to walk to their school near Fond-des-Blancs. The reason some parents still sent their children to the Thomas's school is because their teachers are very well qualified. They have gone through training school, and ours have not.

From fourth grade on up, we have a teacher for every subject. We tried to determine which teachers were at ease in what subject, subsequently making for a fun learning experience for the students. When Joy saw and heard how well the Labaleine students do in the national exams, she said she advised the Labaleine children to attend the Labaleine school.

School in Labaleine!

In the summer of 1994, three teachers from their school who had gone to training school held seminars with our teachers for about a week.

I also heard of a retired certified school inspector in Miragoane who was conducting seminars for teachers. We hired him to come to Labaleine twice a month. He would come on Friday and would work all day Saturday. He drilled our teachers year round for three years. Our teachers were very pleased. This really helped our school, both academically and spiritually. We try to be creative in finding resource people to help us in areas where we need strengthening. I believe our strength is in delegating subjects. Our teachers get in the emotion of learning, and teach with passion.

Our school sent 40 students to take the national exam in the '98–'99 school year and 35 passed. Of the approximately 100 schools in our district, we usually place 2nd or 3rd. My brother Jovin, who is director of the Labaleine school, would like to see us be in 1st place, but I prefer 3rd or 4th. I think first place would make us too vulnerable.

Things are no longer the same with the people in Labaleine and surrounding communities. Today, those that formerly mocked would probably consider moving into Labaleine.

I believe the concept of Christian education that is being integrated by the evangelical churches is working. The concept of a school working together with the church is an excellent way to share the gospel with the unbelievers. It is the dream of every parent to see their children learn how to read and write and further equip themselves for the future. Having a school in a community and providing available resources to train the young minds proves to be an excellent choice and a priceless investment.

It is easy for anyone to give a fish to someone, but it is a difficult task to teach a person how to fish for himself. The challenge of teaching people how to do things on their own is not easy. It becomes more painful when a person must leave a parasitic lifestyle where he or she totally depended on someone else to be the provider. I believe the church can use the school as a tool to provide ways for a self-sustainable lifestyle for the local people.

I believe the people need to be helped out of their "hole," but the key is to fill the hole so they can't fall in again.

19

The News

Miriam Labady called one afternoon to our apartment in Kansas. She said that Eris had planned to call, but he couldn't come to the phone.

At first I thought Eris was hurt, but then she told me that my father had had an accident and did not survive. She also explained that Eris had wanted to call me and break the news about my father's death, but he just couldn't contain himself, so she had done it.

Later I learned that Father was on a trip to a church conference at Carrefour, when he fell off the top of the charcoal truck that he was riding on and landed on his head. Others were with him who knew him and took him to the hospital at Petit Goave. Because of severe head injuries, the hospital staff was unable to give him the care he needed. He was put on another truck and transported to Port-au-Prince, where he later died. This happened on Saturday, January 16, 1984.

After she called about 4 PM, I first called my brother Aurel in

Paris, France, and Pastor Ivan from the church and other friends. Jack Bailey from Tifton wired us some money, and people from Hutchinson helped us buy tickets to fly to Haiti for the funeral.

Aurel arrived in Haiti before I did. He was working in Paris driving cement truck. His plan was to eventually come to Labaleine and help with the work.

I believe we got our tickets on Sunday morning and flew out on Monday. Aurel met us at the airport, and we went to the morgue together to view the body. Our luggage got left behind at Miami, so we stayed at Pastor Christian's house in Delmas 33. On Tuesday, we got our luggage and went to the police station and asked that the driver of the charcoal truck, whose father was a friend of my father and was put in jail for the mishap, be released. Tuesday night we stayed with Rachel's parents in Fontamara on the west side of Port-au-Prince. On Wednesday we picked up the body and left for Labaleine by midafternoon.

We had sent a message with a person traveling from Port-au-Prince to Labaleine to tell the Labaleine people when we were bringing the body. Eris' pickup truck carried the body. Plus we had a minibus that hauled about 20 people. After we made the turn onto the Fond-des-Blancs road, people were crying and waving at the roadside. People knew him very well because he always traveled that road when he went to Miragoane on his mule. It was dark by this time, but people knew the body was coming. It was an emotional experience. Eris recalled how everything seemed to be crying, and even the trees seemed sorrowful.

All those people knew Father through his ministry and good deeds. When my father got food from MUC, he would share it with the community people, making sure everyone got some. He was an unselfish man.

On our way toward Labaleine, as we crested the hill overlooking Miragoane, we met Madam Cedois in her truck and stopped briefly to talk with her. She knew my father very well. She was well known in Fond-des-Blancs and was the only local woman who owned a truck. She had a chauffeur to drive her truck for her for many years.

There were probably 500 people at Mother's house from neighboring villages for the wake, the customary practice of singing all night at the home of the deceased. Father had been dead long enough that the word had spread. If a person died early in the morning, no wake would be necessary because the body usually gets buried the same day. But more time had passed before we and Aurel had been able to arrive.

Everyone crowded in and around the house until sunrise, singing all the gospel songs we could think of and drinking coffee to stay awake.

At daybreak everyone prepared for the funeral, changing clothes at houses nearby. The funeral service was held on Thursday.

Our family wanted to see Father's face, but when I saw it at the morgue in Port-au-Prince, I could hardly recognize it because of the numerous bruises. The funeral directors had kept the body in ice, and since it would deice it was not appropriate to open the casket for the memorial service in Labaleine.

At about 7:30 AM the body was taken to the church. Many people sang and shared memories of Father. With the large number of people, many stood outside during the services. Pastor Eris arranged the services, and he and Warren Cluxton preached. I had met Warren through Son Light Mission when I taught at their school.

After the services at the church, the body was carried to the large above-the-ground concrete tomb behind my mother's house. The wooden casket was slid into the prepared hole and sealed. After the burial, a meal of rice and bean sauce was served at Mother's house.

20

Return

On Saturday Rachel and I, with the help of others, loaded our belongings onto a donkey and walked the five miles to Fond-des-Blancs. Dorlus Labady then took us to Port-au-Prince. We attended Pastor Christian's church on Sunday and flew back to Wichita, Kansas, on Monday. I was working on my dissertation at Hesston. Returning to school and trying to study with all those emotions made concentration very difficult. It affected me for a long time. When we came back to Miami, the airline lady was surprised that we had been allowed to leave Haiti, since I had only an F1 DS visa (Duration of Stay) and, by law, would have had to get a permit to leave. I shouldn't have been able to get back to the States, but God worked it out.

Brother Aurel returned to Paris. In March 1990, Aurel died of a heart attack at age 35. He was a cement truck driver. He and his family had planned to move back to Haiti in the summer of 1990, but this changed their plans, and they are still living in Paris today.

The Path of Faith

A month after Father's funeral, I returned to Haiti with Ervin Stutzman, Jonas P. Yoder, Henry Nisley, and Eli Yoder from Kansas; John Mast from Oklahoma; and Willis Miller from Iowa, to make necessary arrangements in the church since Father's passing.

The church people asked that Pastor Ednor Maignan, who was previously an assistant to my father, be ordained as church leader. We also had communion together. It was decided that Pastor Ednor would report to Pastor Eris. Eris was licensed to perform marriages, so he could help out in that capacity. Pastor Ednor would then be able to serve communion and do baby dedications. Baby dedications are taken after the pattern of Samuel's dedication in the Old Testament. We were no longer under Pastor Ducasse's mission at this time.

Also on this trip we worked on plans for the school building that Father and I had talked about for a long time. Father had died before the dream to have a school in our village had come true.

Even today, as pastor of the church, I make myself accountable to Eris. One is not above the other; it just helps keep us on track.

Today I am senior pastor, with Ednor Maignan, Merisier Maignan, and Bienne Buissereth as assistant pastors and Julne Celestin as evangelist. Julne is in his upper 70s and unable to read or write, therefore unable to assume the office of pastor. He serves communion and does baby dedications and visitations.

In Haiti, one can be a minister in charge and the others work under him. While I was in the States, Pastor Ednor took care of the church. After my father passed away I became responsible. This is what the church wanted.

In Haiti, by law, the pastor needs to have a certain level of education, especially to be able to sign documents. While I was in school in the States, we had Pastor Eris take care of the legal things for Pastor Ednor. When we moved to Haiti in 1993, I held leadership-training seminars for brethren who were recommended by the church to be leaders. We met twice a week at the school in the afternoon for a leadership seminar. In 1996 Ednor Maignan, Merisier Maignan, and Bienne Buissereth were installed as ministers, Ocalipe Celestin and Dieunys Celestin as deacons, and Julne Celestin as evangelist. Pastor Eris and Pastor Jean Thomas were present for the installation.

In Haiti, schools are mostly owned by individuals or churches. Our school is a church school. A mission works with a church, but in a legal sense the church has the authority.

A pastor can, however, perform marriages, conduct funerals, and gather more than 20 people if he works under a licensed pastor.

Over the years I have especially enjoyed working with Pastor Eris Labady and Pastor Jean Thomas. We are within a few years of the same age, and the churches we are responsible for are all within an 8-mile area.

Pastor Eris Labady is two years younger than me. I first met him in Desruisseaux while I was attending St. Jean Baptiste School. He moved to Desruisseaux from Gode, his hometown, to attend Ecole

The Path of Faith

Frère. We worked together in the Miragoane church under Pastor Ducasse and later in Pastor Christian's church in Carrefour. We sang French and Creole songs that Eris wrote in duet and quartet together.

One of the highlights in my relationship with Pastor Eris was when we preached revival meetings together in 1981. We preached in various communities in the Puit Salle area. One Friday morning after a few days of preaching in Puit Salle, a group of people appeared at the door of the church where we were staying. They brought us an ill six-year-old whose oldest sibling had died after showing the same symptoms. Community people and her family thought it came from a spell that was cast on her. Pastor Eris, Pastor Malval Duval, Pastor Ednor Cheri, and I took the girl into a small room in the church building and prayed for about four hours. A few times her whole body would shake and she would roll on the floor, foaming. I watched her closely and noticed that her shaking would begin at her hands, so we held her hands and prayed. Then she slept on her mat on the floor for about an hour. She foamed and rollicked again. We read the Bible and prayed, and she slept again. One of the church ladies came and asked about her condition. After we told her that the girl was resting, she made food for her. Later the girl awoke and ate. The Lord had performed a miracle.

The community people were astounded. The girl's mother had a band around her waist to give her more strength to cry. This told us she had expected her child to die. This was my first encounter with evil spirits.

In the evening we had an open-air meeting in Mouillage Fouquet. We prayed at a few houses before the meeting. Thirteen people were saved that evening. During the Sunday morning services at Puit Salle, the six-year-old stood up and testified of her miraculous healing.

After our family moved to Haiti in 1993, the girl who was healed brought a gift of fried fish in appreciation for that prayer meeting many years earlier.

Today, Pastor Eris and Miriam and their four children live in Petionville, Haiti, and are responsible for the mission work in Puit Salle sponsored by Palm Grove Mennonite Church of Sarasota, Florida. The Labadys are also very involved in the work of Christian Aid Ministries, based in Berlin, Ohio, with a field office in Titanyen, Haiti.

Miriam and Pastor Eris met in Miragoane while Miriam worked at MUC. Miriam went to Haiti in 1969 and worked at the mission for four years before they were married in 1977.

I met Pastor Jean Thomas in the mid-1980s. He and his wife, Joy, and their three sons live near Fond-des-Blancs. The Thomases moved from Jackson, Mississippi, in 1981 after Jean's brother Paul visited Fond-des-Blancs and noticed the need for a church and school program.

Jean grew up in St. Michel de L'Attalaye, Haiti, while Joy is American and was raised in Oregon. They met and married in Jackson, Mississippi. Pastor Jean is responsible for a Baptist church near their home. Through their organization, Haitian Christian Development Foundation, he is involved in many development projects and also has a tree nursery and plants lots of trees. They have an excellent school program that is run by his wife, Joy. They also have a Home Economics program at the school to teach sewing and embroidery.

Jean Thomas, Eris Labady, and I were involved in the rebuilding of 160 miles of roads in the Fond-des-Blancs area through a project sponsored by US/AID. Working on the road provided an excellent income for the local people, employing approximately 1,000 workers.

The three of us, along with Brother Patrick Lataillade, have discussed the possibility of offering vocational education to our larger community. We talked about having an agricultural school in Labaleine, a tech school in Fond-des-Blancs, and a woodworking school in Puit Salle.

Brother Patrick is also very instrumental in evangelization and is encouraging a sweeping move toward indigenous missionaries in Haiti.

The Path of Faith

Father, mid-1960s

Mother

21

Father

Periodically, Father would ride his mule to Miragoane, leaving at 3:30 in the morning to give a report of the church and do business in town. He would stay a full day and be back in the evening. Father would also take local goods such as charcoal and eggs to give to the mission in Miragoane. When I talked with Pastor Ducasse's wife, Yolande, a few years ago, she remembered Father's kindness and his gifts of eggs that he often brought to the mission from our own chickens.

When Father was 17 years old, his father, mother, and one of his brothers all died the same year. Typhoid malaria, the assumed cause of their death, was rampant in the community during this time. Five brothers and one sister remained. It was about this time that Father became a Christian. People had been using water from the same spring that the animals drank from. In 1946, after the spring was captured, the malaria cases lessened.

Father never attended school. Seemingly, others his age didn't go to school either. Even if he had had access to a school, it would have been difficult for Father to find time to attend, since he was the oldest of the children and was responsible for the family.

With my father's help I was able to reap a good education. My father never hesitated about allowing me to go to the States. He was just as excited as I was, maybe even more so. He saw it as a door of opportunity.

When the Church of God in Christ was working with us, Edmond Maignan and Lisoiel Maignan and others were resident leaders in the church. My father assisted them. After Edmond moved to Ebenezer Church and Lisoiel to the Church of God, and later to the Assemblies of God, Father became the leader in the church. Lisoiel later returned to our church and died while attending there.

Father was next in rank as leader under Pastor Lefond Charles and Japhe Pompe, who were from the mother church in La Colline. Japhe was the leader in charge of the church in Labaleine and ordained my father to be his assistant. When the Church of God in Christ leaders did not return after Hurricane Flora, Father became the leader. Father was considered a lay minister. He preached, prayed for the children, and gave counsel. He was, however, not qualified to perform marriages because of his limited reading ability. Other local pastors, including Pastor Christian Maisonneuve and Pastor Eris, helped out by performing marriages. Father was the leader until his death in 1984.

Before my father was ordained, Japhe came nearly every Sunday.

Sometimes he came on Saturday evening and stayed overnight. He was the only regular pastor when our church was with the Church of God in Christ. He was often at our house for lunch before heading home.

Pastor Charles was district leader over Japhe Pompe. Since Japhe was not qualified to serve communion, Pastor Charles would come once a month for that. Someone from Labaleine would take a mule the nine or ten-mile trip to L'homond to pick up Pastor Charles on the Saturday before we had communion. As a matter of respect, the person fetching him would walk while the pastor rode the mule. If no one volunteered, which was rare, someone was assigned to the job. I was too young to go alone, but once I rode the three- or four-hour mule-back trip with my Uncle Edward. On the way back we both walked and Pastor Charles rode. Japhe, who lived six miles away in La Colline, usually came alone on his mule.

I never heard my father read in the church. I think he could only read a limited amount. When I was ten years old, I began reading Scriptures in the Sunday evening services for him while he preached. This was special to me. It made me feel important. He knew numbers very well but his reading of words was limited. At first I didn't read on Sunday mornings because I was too young to take this kind of responsibility in front of the congregation. Even though it may have come haltingly, one of the other men would read for him on Sunday mornings. Sometime after I was baptized at age 16, I started reading on Sunday morning as well.

I remember from the years of working alongside my father that he preached against the concubine lifestyle, a man and woman living together without being married. After people realized the seriousness of this sin, more couples got married first. Father probably found out about this scriptural mandate through Pastor Ducasse and other preachers. In the church today, we still preach against the concubine lifestyle, and we discipline as we believe the Bible commands.

Father wasn't able to sit down and study for himself. His practice of preaching was done mostly by getting me to read Scripture, and then he would expound on what he understood. Without the ability to read, he would ask me to read a certain passage by giving me the reference; he then knew what he wanted to say. This must have been the work of the Holy Spirit.

When a person would come to church, or if my father would go to a person's house to pray and lead someone to Christ, he would recite Matthew 4:10 and 11, and

> *Then saith Jesus unto him, Get thee hence, Satan: for it is written, Thou shalt worship the Lord thy God, and Him only shalt thou serve.*
>
> *Then the devil leaveth him, and, behold, angels came and ministered unto him.*
>
> Matthew 4:10, 11

the person would repeat it after him. After the person was led to Christ and before a final prayer, my father would put his hand on the person's head and gently slap his Bible on top. This was symbolic of casting out the devil. The same Scripture was also used when a discouraged or backslidden person requested prayer, only there was no head slapping.

On communion Sunday, following the message, all members would rise one-by-one to their feet and testify that they were ready to partake of communion.

I remember after Pastor Charles served the communion grape juice and bread, he would have a towel around his waist and would go around with a white basin and wash all our members' and visiting church members' feet himself. Then one of the deacons would wipe them.

After we returned to Haiti in 1993, we drew up guidelines for our church, and included the stipulation that no politician may come into our church to campaign. We got the church committee together and told them that the Bible tells us only one thing to do for politicians. That is to pray for them. That's

> *But shun profane and vain babblings: for they will increase unto more ungodliness. And their word will eat as doth a canker: ...*
> II Timothy 2:16, 17

it. As far as campaigning—that's not our responsibility. They weren't accustomed to that, because in our culture it's a given that we always need to respect people in authority. After we explained what we meant, we got some "amens" from the committee.

22

Back to Georgia

After I received my Associate Degree at Hesston and Rachel completed two-years of courses at Hesston and one year at JUCO, we made plans to move to Georgia to attend the University of Georgia in Athens. They had very good nursing and agricultural programs. We used our Ford Pinto to drag a U-Haul trailer with our belongings.

Wilfred Joseph, a Haitian friend, had been living with us in Hutchinson and moved with us to Georgia. (I had stayed with Wilfred's family the first few months after I moved to Miragoane.) Since Wilfred was with us, we couldn't board at the dorm, so we spent a few days at Days Inn in Atlanta. Instead of sending him off on his own, we decided to find a place where we could be together.

After a few days Wilfred suggested that Mennonites are very nice people and asked why we don't look them up in the phone book. We may be able to arrange boarding with them since we didn't know anyone in the area. He thought we were spending too much money staying at the motel. I found the number for the Berea Mennonite Church and their pastor, Carl Martin. I called the parsonage from the motel.

Carl and his wife, Arlene, visited us at the motel later the same day. After talking briefly, we discovered a connection through Carl's daughter Sharon's boyfriend, Steve Martin, who Rachel had met at Rosedale Bible Institute. We had also stayed with Steve Martin's family two years earlier on our trip with Willis Miller, promoting Water for Life.

Carl suggested we unload our belongings into the church basement and return the U-Haul. Sharon, the Martins' daughter, went to stay at her sister's house, allowing Wilfred to use her room. Another daughter, Kathy, moved to the same bedroom as her parents and gave Rachel and me her bedroom. This was certainly an extreme measure of kindness from the Martins. Kathy became like a sister to us.

We spent over a month at the Martins, until we were able to rent at the Morrow College apartment complex. We never did attend the University of Georgia as we had planned.

At the motel we had seen a report on TV about a group of Haitian refugees in the Atlanta area. We called the TV station, and they gave us a phone number for the refugee director. According to the TV report, we knew that the refugees were staying close to the capitol building in Atlanta, so we headed in that direction. When we drove past Central Presbyterian where the TV interview was conducted, I saw a man who looked like a Haitian standing on the sidewalk. First I spoke in English, but when I heard his broken speech, I asked if he knew Creole. I asked him where the Haitians were meeting for services. He introduced himself as Jacque Romain Joseph, the pastor's brother, and said they were meeting in the building behind him. We joined the small congregation for worship. This was the beginning of a long, fulfilling relationship with the Haitian Ministry Theophile Church in Christ in Atlanta.

Later Romain Joseph's brother, Roland, the current pastor of the church, said it didn't make sense why he was walking around outside—he should have been teaching his Sunday school class. It was during the break between Sunday school and worship that Romain was outside and coincidently we came along. Or are there coincidences with God?

We became members at the Haitian Ministry church, and later Rachel and I became involved in their youth ministry and taught youth Sunday school class. Haitian Ministry helped me get my Green Card for easier travel between Haiti and the States.

Rachel continued her prerequisites at Clayton State College in Morrow, while I worked in the receiving department at the Fort Gilem army base warehouse. At the warehouse we supplied clothing to army base personnel worldwide. We spent three years in Morrow.

About a year after we bought the Ford Pinto car, we noticed a crack in the motor. I got an estimate to have it repaired, but it cost so much we discussed getting another vehicle instead. For a long time, I had dreamed of having a Honda Accord. So we traded the Pinto.

Soon after we had the Accord, I dreamed one night that I was going up a very steep mountain in Haiti. Three-fourths of the way up, the Honda stalled. I braked. I couldn't go forward and I didn't want to go down with it. I eased out of the car, keeping my foot on the brake. After I was out, I released the brake. My dear Honda went rolling down the mountainside. Now I was without my car, but I was able to travel on foot and continue up the mountain. This vision was a lesson to me to not attach myself to material things. They can entangle you.

In 1986, before Rachel was able to finish her nursing school at Clayton State College in Morrow, our first son, Samuel, was born.

23

Florida

While I worked at the military warehouse in Morrow, Walter Sawatzky, whom I had met in Haiti in the 1980s, invited me to come to Miami, Florida, to work with the youth from the Haitian churches in Miami-Dade County. In 1987, after I was injured at the warehouse and unable to work, we moved to Miami. It was difficult for us to leave behind our friends at Haitian Ministry church, but it seemed to be the best thing for us to do.

I also helped do surveys of the 130 Haitian churches in Miami-Dade County through Latin American Missions, where Walter was also involved. I talked to about 200 pastors, asking them questions about their ministry. We tried to determine their needs so we could better equip the churches by providing courses or materials to meet those needs.

Leonard Burkholder, whom I met at Rosedale Bible Institute, surveyed the Anglo churches, and I was responsible for the Haitian churches. In the two or three years of surveys, I made contacts with over 130 churches. I traveled around on Sunday to set up appointments because that seemed to be the easiest time to find the pastors. If it worked out, I did the survey on the first encounter. The session took about half an hour. I really enjoyed surveying the Haitian churches. I love to ask questions and learn.

During the surveys in Miami, I noticed many of the churches had only 50-100 attendees with one pastor, and many were renting their church buildings. Haitian Ministry in Atlanta had about eight pastors and 300 attendees. I talked to Pastor Roland Joseph from the Atlanta church and asked him to come meet with the Miami pastors in November 1988. I thought a few small churches should join and form one larger congregation. This would reduce the renting costs per member, and there would be more pastors to share the ministry. Having four or five pastors and delegating responsibilities, we thought, would better meet the needs of the church people. We offered the idea, but they didn't buy it.

Speakers at the seminar included Pastor Felix Jean Guillaume and Pastor Roland Joseph. They talked about pastors working together in the church and making it successful. After renting for a number of years, Haitian Ministry in Atlanta had bought a church building and parsonage. They exceeded the required payments on their mortgage, and at the end of ten years the building was paid off completely.

The church is completely run by Haitians, with no American church involved. Some of the church people had moved to Atlanta from Haiti, and some had relocated from New York.

Another meeting of Haitian leaders was held in October 1989 in Little Haiti in Miami, Florida. The guest speakers were Pastor Eris Labady from Haiti and Pastor Roland Joseph from Atlanta. Concerns were raised of a need for a Christian library and Bible school for pastors who did not have the privilege of attending seminary. A committee was formed to implement the projects.

Haitian Bible Institute opened its doors in February 1991 with 11 students and four teachers. Dr. Alain Rocourt, Pastor Rodolph Neact, Pastor Jacques Saint-Louis, Robert Cheri, and I taught at the Institute. By February 1999, the second group of students had graduated, making a total of 19 graduates.

The Haitian Bible Institute, with its own board of directors, began operations with a seed grant from World Vision. The Institute, with two branches, one for youth training and one for leadership training, serves as a miniseminary.

Haitian Bible Institute is open year-round. Our goal was to bring students to a level where they could be accepted in the Excel program at Miami Christian College, where they could pursue almost any college major they chose.

Another project with Haitian Bible Institute was the youth ministry under MCC with a correspondence Bible course that I took to various churches. At one time there were over 100 Haitian and American students taking the course. The courses were offered in English and French. The courses were geared toward practicing and aspiring church leaders.

The Path of Faith

Before the Bible course ministry I also conducted Sunday afternoon youth meetings with two Haitian churches.

I once dreamed there were two students who were attending the Institute with me in Labaleine, on the top of the mountain behind my mother's house. There are no houses up there, but the students and I were in a mud-plastered house with electricity. With a loudspeaker I called out to the people of Labaleine to turn on their lights. The whole valley lit up, and I noticed a big asphalt highway down through the center of the valley, with pole lights along the side. I didn't notice any doors or windows in the house, and I didn't see any bulbs, but the house was filled with light. I don't know if this will someday be true for Labaleine or not.

Through Walter Sawatzky, I also worked at World Vision as a small-business consultant. They wanted me to seek out small businesses and offer them advice if needed and to offer financial assistance to get their businesses started. The program was geared toward minorities.

For two and a half years I worked at Little Haiti Housing with David Harder, founder and administrator of the organization. The Little Haiti community is a section of Miami with a great concentration of Haitian residents. According to research done in the early 80s of the community, it was discovered that this area's average income was less than half compared to the rest of Miami. This prompted the development of Little Haiti Housing with the goal of making housing affordable and attainable. About a year after David had started on his own, I was able to help out by bridging the culture and language gap to make house ownership a reality for many people. David was responsible for the construction and business side, and I worked on the marketing and training, and we worked together through trial and error to develop the Little Haiti Housing program.

Individuals who proved worthy and were accepted by a bank for a loan were given a six-week classroom-setting preparatory course. Once graduated, we would find a suitable house for them to buy. This was a very interesting experience, and it was very encouraging to work with David Harder.

Our second son, Gardel, was born in November 1987. In the fall of 1988, Rachel enrolled at Florida International University. Rachel graduated in December 1990, two years after we moved to Miami. What a great day for her!

One of Rachel's classmates was on reserve in the army and got a four-year degree in nursing at Miami. Rachel was offered a $5,000 sign-up bonus to be a nurse for the army. If we hadn't had a vision to return to Haiti, we would probably have considered that. It would not have involved combat. She would have been helping people.

Rachel was invited to many dinners of groups who were recruiting young nursing students. Various organizations offered from $5,000 up to $10,000 as a sign-up bonus.

After Rachel graduated from Miami, she began working for an agency that hired nurses for $12 per hour. To get her license, Rachel needed to take the State Board test. She whipped it on the second try. After she had her license, her wage increased to $24 per hour. Jokingly, I told her this was enough for us to not return to Haiti. However, we both felt a strong tug to return.

Rachel worked in three Miami hospitals and worked a lot with Cuban people and was able to improve her Spanish, which she had begun in high school in Haiti.

After Samuel and Gardel were born, and Rachel was still attending at Florida International University, I took them with me on the road. They went along when I surveyed the Haitian churches and also while I worked with Little Haiti Housing.

While in Miami I attended Miami Christian College and graduated from the Excel program with a bachelor's degree in Human Resource Management.

24

Pearl of the Antilles

I'm sure people from our community are involved in voodoo, but I have never seen public appearances of it in Labaleine. When I read textbooks or go to the library, I carry a red highlighter with me. When I see voodoo connected to Haiti, I take my red highlighter over the word "voodoo," symbolizing that the blood of Christ has covered it. It has to be a red highlighter; pink won't do.

There have been discussions that intimated that Haiti was dedicated to Satan. It's true that voodoo was widespread in Haitian society—but that was then, and this is now. For those people, that was their period. Today is our period. This is our generation and we are responsible for today. Haiti belongs to us, not them. Those people are dead. I don't speak that language anymore.

I think it's about time to bury the idea that voodoo and Haiti go together. Community people tried to have a cockfight arena in Labaleine. It worked for a short time, then it lost out. Labaleine belongs to the Lord, not to any of Satan's activities. Even the Catholic

The Path of Faith

church cannot work its way through, despite their numerous attempts. Our goal is to reach everyone in Labaleine for the Lord and make the community a Christian community, where the Name of the Lord can be exalted. I even refuse to consider voodoo a part of my culture. Jesus Christ is the foundation of my culture.

In 1998 I was teaching the men's Sunday school class in the church, and we came up with the idea of claiming Labaleine for the Lord. We were planning to have a march, but instead, we stood in a circle. In April 1998 all the local churches joined in dedication of our community to the Lord. More than 200 people formed a hand-in-hand circle. I think we should still have a march sometime.

My heart is burdened for the young people. I want to educate the youth, and then eventually Catholicism and cockfights will fade away. That's my crusade. I'm hoping that within my lifetime voodoo in Haiti will be barely heard of. We are headed in that direction.

I've seen a voodoo temple near the Leogane children's home. It is one of the ugliest and filthiest places around.

There is a name for Haiti and it's not voodoo—it's "the pearl of the Antilles." Because of its lush tropical forests, Haiti was at one time considered the pearl of the West Indies islands. Today, Haiti has a lot to offer. I think the "pearl" part is returning. I believe we have a lot of potential, and we need to go to the heart of the people and get the ball rolling again.

25

Coffee, Sisal, Goats

Three farming commodities that I really want to push at the school are coffee, sisal, and goats. Goats have two kids per year. Each one brings about $50 (Htn.) at the market, and there is demand for the meat. Also, a goat is not as big as a cow and doesn't need to be led to the spring for water—they get their moisture from feeding on vegetation—which simplifies their upkeep.

Sisal is a plant with great potential in Haiti. I hope that someday we can arrange to export sisal to the States to make twine. We have already planted over 1,000 plants.

While we lived in Pennsylvania, I read in a newspaper where a man in the States was selling coffee for 15 or 16 years without one coffee plant on his land. His gross income was about $17 million per year from coffee alone. I took the article to Labaleine and had a parents meeting at the school. I showed them the picture and asked them to describe what they saw. After they said it is coffee in the man's hand, I asked them how much they think he makes on his coffee per year. Some guessed $500, $1,000, $2,000. One guessed $5,000. I told them that he's making $17 million per year, and we are not! I told them this man cannot grow a coffee tree in his country, but we can! I explained to them that coffee doesn't grow in the U.S. because of the climate.

Coffee cannot be raised in the United States, I told them, but there is a coffee pot wherever you go—motels, restaurants, workplaces. We found out that coffee is the number two imported product in America, after fuel. So what are we doing? Canada doesn't have one coffee tree. England doesn't have a tree. France doesn't have a tree. Spain doesn't have a tree. Japan doesn't have a tree. Russia doesn't have a tree. China doesn't have a tree. These are superpower countries that love coffee, but they don't have the climate to grow it. We do. I told them to wake up and smell the coffee.

I told the students the superpower countries are asking for coffee, coffee, coffee. I put out a paper for the students to sign their name if they were interested in planting coffee. On one day I got more than 100 signatures.

After that meeting it seemed everyone was asking for coffee trees. The old-timers in the community found out about it and began giving me advice about raising coffee. I know the coffee idea works, but I am glad for their input because I'm looking for human resources to make it happen. Several people came and asked me to use their land. The school has leased some land for ten years that will provide funds for its landowner plus provide work for other locals. Several people came to me and said, "My land is available, my land is available."

A coffee tree bears in 2½ years and has about 10 branches. Every branch has about 13 knots and every knot has a cluster of 10 beans. Every year more branches are added. A coffee tree lasts between 60 and 70 years. There are still coffee plants toward the village of Kay Chalin that were there when I was a boy. And they are still bearing.

Goat

The Path of Faith

Samuel

Gardel

Raphael

26

Back and Forth

When we moved from Georgia to Florida in 1987, we stayed at Ed and Eva Eby's house in Miami Shores for about a month. In 1991 we bought a house in Miami Shores, where we lived until we moved back to Haiti in 1993. Our youngest son, Raphael, was born in August 1992. Before we returned to Haiti, Rachel and I and our three boys made a special trip to Pennsylvania to express our appreciation to John Strickler and his wife, Erma, and the Old Order River Brethren for all they had done to help us through school. They rejoiced with us.

I remember when I would call John Strickler and tell him that school is going to start and asked if he was able to help, he would ask how much we needed and said the check is in the mail. He never scratched his head when we called him to tell him that a bill was due. Myron Dietz, a member of the River Brethren community who also helped us with our schooling, was very pleased that we returned to Haiti to help our own people.

By 1992 my dear wife had come to the States, learned English, become a registered nurse, and borne three boys—all in ten years time.

As we had promised ourselves, after Rachel and I reached our educational goals in the States, we returned to Labaleine in 1993. Thanks to Ervin Stutzman, the clinic building had been started in the previous year, and Rachel immediately began serving the medical needs of the community. I pastored the church and served as administrator in the school.

Our family moved into the top story of the clinic building.

The return to Labaleine gave me a feeling of responsibility and fulfillment. I felt a responsibility to share what I had learned with those who didn't have the opportunity that I had. While I was growing up, I didn't expect to one day provide leadership for the younger generation. Watching the community children doing their daily chores and playing their games stirred memories of my own childhood. Their games, however, were more advanced. While I was growing up, we spun tops and kicked oranges and grapefruits and sometimes a tennis ball. Now the boys were playing soccer.

Today, I receive a great sense of satisfaction and fulfillment to see the great number of children attending the Labaleine school. Some of them are among the top students in the country. With God all things are possible.

Our family visited Pastor Ducasse at Miragoane to express my thanks to him for helping me. We spent some special moments together. I told him that we were working in Labaleine, continuing the work of my father, and he was happy to hear that. Pastor Ducasse died in March 1999.

Ervin and Emma Stutzman have been involved in Labaleine over a period of more than 14 years. I personally give my heartfelt thanks for all their efforts and their undaunting desire to see the Labaleine community flourish.

Today, the mission is supported by Haitian Relief and Missions, Inc., with executive board members in Ohio and Kansas and an American couple in administration in Labaleine.

We, the people of Labaleine, give our heartfelt thanks to the many supporters of the Haiti Benefit Auctions held throughout the year. Funds from these auctions have been extremely helpful in the development of our village and giving our people access to many valuable resources. Thank you, brothers and sisters.

In 1998, we decided to temporarily move back to the United States with the goal of having the boys continue their education in the States. We moved to Lancaster, Pennsylvania, and my mother joined us.

In June 2000 we moved to Morrow, Georgia, a suburb of Atlanta. I am involved in the children's ministry of Haitian Ministry Theophile Church in Christ and work for Delta Airlines. Rachel is a floor nurse in the cardiac unit at Southern Regional Hospital.

In 1986, when I first became a U.S. resident, I wanted to help my father and mother also visit the States. My father died before I got the chance to take him. My mother's first visit to the States was in 1995.

Today it is harder for Haitians to get visas to travel to America or other countries than it was when I got mine. It is probably the result of persons violating their visas.

27

Perspectives on Haitian Life

There is more to Haitian life than poverty. Suicide is unheard of. Americans have high expectations—winning the lottery, getting a new car, getting a new house; and if it doesn't happen, they give up. In Haiti, people have expectations, too; but if it doesn't happen, they say *Demen si Die vle* ("Tomorrow, if it is God's will"). There is a Haitian proverb—*With patience, you will see the udder of bugs.* In other words, anything can happen if you can wait on it. This proverb probably came from slavery days. Historically, Haitians have experienced the work of patience, having lived in slavery and being sold, and seeing this come to an end. I think they were able to see the work of patience, and this concept has been passed from one generation to the next, as shown by this proverb.

I don't believe the slavery mentality has been totally banished. Even though I feel it is slowly fading away, too much of that mentality still exists; we just have different masters. Instead of foreigners being the masters, the local people are. More than from a history of slavery, this mentality probably comes from the different status levels in our country. To me, this servant/master thinking is very evil.

I have this as my motto—I feel that anyone who is living on earth is not living his life to the fullest until he brings his brother or sister up to his level. The reason I say this is because otherwise you will always live in fear of the other person. The fear of him robbing you or killing you because you have so much and he has so little. When everyone is on the same level, you have something to eat, I have something to eat; you have a car, I have a car; you work, I work. There is no fear because we are on the same level.

One concern I have is that illiteracy needs to be stamped out. It blessed me some time ago when I went to Haiti when Madam Alvincy, a sister from the Labaleine church, and her two daughters stood up in church and sang a song together. The way it was sung, it could have been sung anywhere in the world. A man could have come with a trillion dollars and said, "Here, Joel, this is the worth of that." I would say, "No, there is no price tag on that." When I heard that singing, it gave me goose bumps down my back. Each one of the girls was holding a songbook, *reading*, singing beside her mother. This was the fulfillment of a dream.

Our motto in Labaleine is that we want to have everyone believe they are important and to be able to step forward in society. I hope we can eventually share our dream and program with surrounding communities.

The mentality that the slave lady can wash our feet or that the slave man or lady can have our leftovers can be cast into the depths of the sea.

Everybody, whether black or white, rich or poor, enjoys a free ride at times even though it doesn't boost their self-worth. If there are things to be distributed, I believe there should be a plan. When there is no hurricane or emergency, I believe people should be able to work and earn their living. This doesn't allow the beggar mentality to take root. The first step, I believe, is being able to read and think by ourselves, and being able to discuss our interests and feelings.

I think it is a blessing if wherever we go, we respect people for their thinking and base our working relationship on this foundation. Haitians want to work and improve their lives. In our school we pass out school bundles once a year, and this I consider okay, but to pass out goods to the whole community—this is forbidden in Labaleine. I believe the best thing a mission can do in Haiti is to work with the local people, making financial help available as needed for such things as land and housing developments. I believe the best way to help is to pose as an assistant to the locals.

A dream I have is to get the local people involved in a project that they can do themselves. This is something I am striving for. I hope the Lord will allow me to do that before I die. I believe the local people can restore the potential of the soil and make it productive.

We're not looking for handouts. We all need emergency help in time of need, but after that we need to have a structure in place and work together as Christians and support one another.

Today I see myself as a bridge-builder between the States and Haiti. I believe that in Haiti we have the will, and I'm trying to market that will. Stateside Christians like to see when the local people are trying to do things on their own, not only financially, but spiritually as well. They like to hear that the locals are making progress on their own.

David said, "I have been young, and now am old; yet have I not seen the righteous forsaken, nor his seed begging bread." (Psalm 37:25).

I believe the Haitians lack in two areas—rain and financial resources—to get them started. I have a passion burning within me that one day, we, the people of Labaleine, can say, "This year we want you, our supporters, to take a break from whatever you have been doing; we want to pay the bills." I want to see this happen. It's in my bones.

The local people would pay the teachers and grow the food for the school canteen. I think we can. I believe first we need to commit everything to the Lord and second, do it! It's a dream and I believe it can be realized.

28

The Vision

As Haitians, I believe we need to reform education and evangelization in Haiti. The way that academics and the gospel have been presented in recent times was from foreign sources, and our people have had to adapt to it. A goal of local churches now is to reevangelize and reeducate Haiti. We can work in partnership with foreign churches and missionaries, but I don't think it is necessary that all the needs for evangelization have to be provided by foreign missionaries.

Our goal now is to focus on using local resources in Haiti to get the work done. At the same time, we want to keep our partnership with foreign missionaries, because we know that God called us all. He called the American, the Canadian, the French, and the English, as well as the Haitians, to evangelize the world. We have a global work.

We don't have to wait until foreign missionaries come to tell us of a certain way to preach. Since we are able to read and write, we need to engage ourselves in preaching and evangelization. We don't have to wait on Americans to bring clothes. We can work and buy our own clothes. We don't have to wait on the Americans to bring food. We can work and provide our own food. Why should someone beg for bread when he can be taught how to raise rice, or how to raise coffee?

In addition, our people can even go to America and preach the gospel. God has made provision for this. Yes, the people are poor, but God didn't create any poor people except those who are poor in spirit before Him. God created us in His image.

When the locals want something from the mission in Labaleine, they have to buy it. They don't need to pay a lot for it, but they have to buy it. We're not going to raise a generation of beggars. I feel it is 'so far, so good.' But we want to go farther. We want to plant mangoes, coffee, and other things.

There's some land near Fond-des-Blancs that I would like to use to raise food for the community. It is not being used for anything. If we can't raise rice, we could raise bananas or beans or sweet potatoes.

The Bible says that man shall not live by bread alone. Bread is included but is not just handed out; you have to work for it. Preaching the gospel is good, but what's next? I believe as the people of Haiti, our needs go beyond that. We still see the need of partnering. We can share how we've experienced Christ in our lives, just as the Americans have shared their lives with us.

The Vision

I think the Haitian people are waking up right now. I see a new and refreshing concept floating among the leaders in the church in Atlanta. The pastors have come to the point where they're asking for help. They understand that 'he needs me—I need him.' 'He can do something well, so I need him. I can do something well, so he needs me.' I believe when we come to the point where we need each other, that's when it's going to work. The proud know-it-all attitude that came from the slavery/master mentality is vanishing. The Bible tells us that if we will seek the Lord with our whole heart, we will find Him. I believe this is what is happening.

I'm glad that the Haitian church leaders, in the States and in Haiti, are waking up right now to the fact that they are responsible for bringing a change in the educational system in Haiti. The church must participate by investing time, money, and prayer. We don't want a generation of people who go from bad to worse.

In the 2000 Convention in Atlanta, a pastor from Haiti attended and brought a contribution from his church in Haiti to help with expenses at the convention.

I think it's time that when we have Haiti Benefit Auctions in the States, Haitian churches should send their contributions as well. Why not? It may not be much; but whatever it is, we need to send what we can. It doesn't matter if it's one *gourde* or one dollar. I don't like the business of doing all the *getting*. What about the Haitians, what work have we done?

When we, the receivers, start putting back what we have re-

The Path of Faith

ceived—when we start telling our brothers and sisters in the U.S., Canada, or France that we have received this much from you this year; this is what we want to do in return. Then I believe that people in the U.S. and other countries would feel blessed and say, "Yes, this is working."

In 1964, when I was 13 years old, Manius, a man from Labaleine and a friend of my father, and I were traveling the six-mile trip on mule to the beach of the Carribean Sea to get sand to redo the foundation of our house. Manius, who was in his early thirties, had stayed at our house after the hurricane. He was a father figure to me. If my father would send me out, he would trust Manius to go with me.

Just past the village of Gachelin, I was humming old-time gospel songs and suddenly found myself in an ecstasy. My eyes were closed, but I could hear myself and I was in a spirit of worship. What I saw I will never forget.

For about 20 minutes I was singing with a large multitude of people, all different colors, who were standing with me. When I opened my eyes, my mule was still going, following the road, and I was still sitting on my *panno* grass mat on his back. I felt refreshed. I felt blessed.

In recent years the vision has flashed back, and I'm currently nurturing it and want to see it come to reality. I would like to establish a Christian school system where I can reach about 5,000 Haitian students from our area and from the surrounding communities for the Lord. I told the Lord I wouldn't beg for any money—He has to make it happen. I would like to accomplish that for Him before He takes me home.

From the bottom up

CONCLUSION

Many, many people have had an impact on my life, and I hope that mention of them in this book will in a small way give recognition to what they have done. It would be impossible for me to fully repay all the persons who have been there for me over and over. This has been a path of faith in God, but Almighty God uses people to fulfill some of His work. I give my heartfelt thank you to all friends, past and present, mentioned and unmentioned, that have been and will be used in the life of our family. I trust God has blessed you and will bless you fully in heaven for sharing your love.